Tragedy and Philosophy

Social and Critical Theory

A CRITICAL HORIZONS BOOK SERIES

Editorial Board

John Rundell (*University of Melbourne*)
Danielle Petherbridge (*University College Dublin*)
Jeremy Smith (*Federation University*)
Jean- Philippe Deranty (*Macquarie University*)
Robert Sinnerbrink (*Macquarie University*)

International Advisory Board

William Connolly (*Johns Hopkins University, Baltimore*)
Manfred Frank (*Universität Tübingen*)
Leela Gandhi (*La Trobe University, Melbourne*)
Agnes Heller † (*The New School for Social Research in New York*)
Dick Howard (*SUNY at Stony Brook*)
Martin Jay (*University of California, Berkeley*)
Richard Kearney (*Boston College*)
Paul Patton (*University of New South Wales, Sydney*)
Michel Wieviorka (*L'École des Hautes Etudes en Sciences Sociales, Paris*)

VOLUME 26

The titles published in this series are listed at *brill.com/sct*

Tragedy and Philosophy

A Parallel History

By

Agnes Heller[†]

Edited by

John Grumley, David Roberts and Pauline Johnson

With an introduction by

John Grumley and David Roberts

BRILL

LEIDEN | BOSTON

Library of Congress Cataloging-in-Publication Data

Names: Heller, Agnes, author. | Grumley, John E., editor, writer of
  introduction. | Roberts, David, 1937- editor, writer of introduction. |
  Johnson, Pauline, 1953-, editor.
Title: Tragedy and philosophy : a parallel history / by Agnes Heller ;
  edited by John Grumley, David Roberts and Pauline Johnson ; with an
  introduction by John Grumley and David Roberts.
Description: Leiden ; Boston : BRILL, [2021] | Series: Social and critical
  theory, 1572-459X ; 26 | Includes index. | Summary: "This book is the sum
  of Agnes Heller's reflections on European history and culture, seen
  through the prism of Europe's two unique literary creations: tragedy and
  philosophy"– Provided by publisher.
Identifiers: LCCN 2021001676 (print) | LCCN 2021001677 (ebook) |
  ISBN 9789004460058 (hardback) | ISBN 9789004460126 (ebook)
Subjects: LCSH: Tragedy. | European drama (Tragedy)–History and criticism. |
  Philosophy, European–History.
Classification: LCC PN1892 .H385 2021 (print) | LCC PN1892 (ebook) |
  DDC 809.9/162–dc23
LC record available at https://lccn.loc.gov/2021001676
LC ebook record available at https://lccn.loc.gov/2021001677

Typeface for the Latin, Greek, and Cyrillic scripts: "Brill." See and download: brill.com/brill-typeface.

ISSN 1572-459X
ISBN 978-90-04-46005-8 (hardback)
ISBN 978-90-04-46012-6 (e-book)

Copyright 2021 by Agnes Heller, John Grumley, David Roberts and Pauline Johnson. Published by Koninklijke Brill NV, Leiden, The Netherlands.
Koninklijke Brill NV incorporates the imprints Brill, Brill Hes & De Graaf, Brill Nijhoff, Brill Rodopi, Brill Sense, Hotei Publishing, mentis Verlag, Verlag Ferdinand Schöningh and Wilhelm Fink Verlag.
Koninklijke Brill NV reserves the right to protect this publication against unauthorized use. Requests for re-use and/or translations must be addressed to Koninklijke Brill NV via brill.com or copyright.com.

This book is printed on acid-free paper and produced in a sustainable manner.

Contents

Acknowledgements VII

Introduction 1
  John Grumley and David Roberts
  1 The Spirit of Agnes Heller 1
  2 Philosophy and Drama 4
  3 Agnes Heller's Commitment to the Future 6

1 Tragedy and Philosophy 8
  1 What Do Tragedy and Philosophy Have in Common? 8
  2 Tragedy: Its Conditions and Constituents 18
  3 Shakespeare: Tragedy and History 33
  4 French Classicism: Tragedy and Passion 40

2 Drama and Philosophy 47
  1 Bourgeois Drama 47
  2 Drama and Classical German Philosophy 56
  3 Modern Drama and Radical Philosophy 65
  4 The Will to Tragedy and Naturalism 73
  5 Ibsen and Chekhov 81
  6 Sartre and Brecht 90

3 The Endgame of Drama and Philosophy 95
  1 Hegel and the End of History 95
  2 Drama and Philosophy: The Endgame 104

Conclusion 121

Acknowledgements

Shortly before she died Agnes Heller emailed this essay to John Grumley. At the time, he was editing a series of her public lectures given around the world in her last years, published in 2020 as *Afterthoughts Beyond the 'System' Political and Cultural Lectures*. She didn't give specific instructions with respect to the manuscript. We are grateful to her son, György Feher who gave his permission to publish the manuscript and also to John Rundell who agreed to include this book in his series with Brill, *Social and Critical Theory* and his assistance with the final version of the manuscript.

Introduction

John Grumley and David Roberts

1   The Spirit of Agnes Heller

Before her sudden death at Lake Balaton in the country outside Budapest and in the course of editing *Occasional Political and Cultural Lectures: Beyond the 'System'* Agnes Heller emailed John Grumley a long essay which is the content of the present book. Rereading the manuscript and preparing its publication we were struck by the intellectual energy and vitality that had sustained her through a very long life and some of the darkest events and times of the 20th century.

Heller's parallel history of drama and philosophy condenses and concentrates the key interests that have preoccupied her all her life. These are ethics, modernity, literature and the history of philosophy. She tells us in her *A Short History of My Philosophy* how as a young teenager during the last year of the Second World War she turned from wonder at the world to the question of human evil and the explanation of the mass murder of so many of her fellow Jews, friends as well as her father during the events of the Holocaust in Hungary during 1944 and 1945. From the early days in Budapest as a Lecturer at the University of Budapest her first efforts sought to develop a theory of ethics and pose the question of how to be moral. This quickly became a decisive political issue in the face of the totalitarian Soviet-dominated Communist Parties in Eastern Europe, which generated a more oppositional humanist interpretation of Marx under the influence of György Lukács. The Eastern European oppositional voices also included attempts to rehabilitate the idea of conscious subjects as active historical agents who could express freedom and free choice.

Heller was compelled to leave Hungary in 1977 after being dismissed from her academic position for the second time and forced to live by translations. A ban on publication and continuing political harassment led to the decision to emigrate to Australia with her husband Ferenc Fehér and their son György, and György together with Maria Márkus and their two sons.

In Australia Heller began a series of books that develop a new theory of modernity. At the height of the Cold War and rising nuclear tension she proposed a more sophisticated understanding of the dynamics of modernity that replaced the opposition between liberal capitalism and communism or socialism with a new model of multiple logics, political, economic, and technological and rational ones, countervailing and supporting each other. On this basis, Heller believed this model would better comprehend the evolutionary historical processes and the political future. In her last decades she returned, not exclusively but mainly to her first love – literature and the higher cultural forms. Agnes Heller had not only read or seen most of Shakespeare's great works on the stage but could quote long passages from the dialogues. This devotion is everywhere evident in this parallel history. Such enthusiasm and knowledge inform her history of the evolution of drama from the ancient classical tradition to modernity.

In respect to philosophy, Agnes Heller's late works and essays were torn by seemingly opposed inspirations. One was the classical tradition of the history of philosophy and especially Hegel's philosophy of history and the idea of the 'end of history' and the wisdom of the 'Owl of Minerva.' It is worth remembering that in her last years she was writing a three-volume history of philosophy just like the old Hegel. Despite this dedication to tradition, her works of the 1990's includes *A Philosophy of History In Fragments*. Her understanding of the modern history of philosophy focused on the series of crises that followed Hegel and needed to be incorporated into a more complex historical narrative from a contemporary post-modern perspective: the critique of purely 'contemplative' philosophy in Feuerbach's and Marx's 'materialism' and later by Kierkegaard and Nietzsche. Initially this crisis was instigated by the turn to the critical and practical meaning of philosophy with Feuerbach and Marx in the wake of the historical changes after the Napoleonic Wars, followed by another turn to inwardness in the works of Nietzsche and Kierkegaard. In both cases, Heller speaks of a series of 'blood transfusions' because the fragmentation of modernity summoned new vocabularies and perspectives as the course of the 19th century unfolded.

Nietzsche's critique of Plato's Socratic rationalism and objectivity is supplemented by the emphasis on the irrational and subjectivity. Nietzsche's return to the pre-Socratics and Kierkegaard's exploration of a new transcendental, normative perspective and philosophical forms and expression reveal that Hegel's 'Owl of Minerva' was nothing like a stationary contemplative wisdom of the 'end of history.' It was transformed into the 'bird of paradise' that has taken flight, to move with the inspiration of the times and accept new challenges and new answers to the present.

Agnes Heller's approach is evident in her story of the course of the history of philosophy in the 20th century up to the present. The radical philosophers of the 19th century gave way to a new generation of revolutionaries: Husserl, Heidegger, Wittgenstein, Foucault and Derrida: each responds to their immediate ancestors and to the times. The twentieth century to which they were responding gave rise to new historical fragmentations: cultural, scientific and philosophical. The post-First World War philosophical world in Europe is characterised by new divisions: new sciences like sociology and political science, the mathematization of the natural sciences and the division of philosophy into new schools like analytical philosophy and existentialism.

Husserl reflects these dramatic social and cultural changes. On the hand, Husserl continues the deconstruction of Cartesian metaphysics while preserving the Cartesian programme to provide ultimate, absolute foundations and a true science. The deconstruction of traditional philosophy is further prosecuted in Wittgenstein's work on the philosophy of language. His later work on ordinary language and forms of life tends to render traditional epistemology obsolete. This attention to the ordinary and to 'forms of life' has a tendency to focus on that which is unique and undermines the transcendental. Heidegger turn to *Dasein* in *Being and Time* is another and earlier version of the same trend. This is continued by contemporary philosophers like Habermas and Gadamer who emphasise the communicative dimension of language and prejudice. However, with Habermas, the tension always evident in Heller between tradition and its fragmentation and innovation is also obvious in his development of a Kantian-style 'universal pragmatism,' based in living empirical communities, which hopes to rescue of reason and rational argument from the perceived dangers of historical relativism.

Another instance of this tension is Adorno and Horkheimer's critique in their *Dialectic of Enlightenment*. Despite Adorno's ongoing critique of instrumental reason and the alienated rationality of mass society and his artistic preference for new cultural forms and aphorist style, Heller still sees him as standing close to the thinkers of the Enlightenment. Similar negative and positive stances towards the Enlightenment are traced through the works of Michel Foucault and Jacques Derrida. She met both in New York, discussed their ideas and even co-taught with Derrida at the New School before he died. Heller views Foucault as a son of the 20th century: a hetero-interpreter, driven by a desire to overturn traditional approaches to issues of power and knowledge. At the same time, Heller recalls that on the occasion of taking up his chair at the *College de France* Foucault said that we could not overcome Hegel. Similarly, Heller interprets Derrida as an omnivorous hermeneutician who has gone one step further than Foucault in making everything a text. But even more than this, there are no standpoints or messages in texts, since standpoints and messages deconstruct themselves while you are reading them: 'no final results and no final consequences can be drawn.' In this sentence one can feel Heller's excitement and endorsement that 'every text is a goldmine!' Yet even in philosophy as interpretation the tension remains. Today there are no philosophical schools and significant philosophies have become personal. Derrida's philosophy was a personal one that has passed with him. For Heller, this is the last "goodbye" for philosophy.

2 Philosophy and Drama

Agnes Heller proposes a 'parallel history' of drama and philosophy that stretches from fourth-century Athens to the 20th century. It is not a continuous history, however, but a story of the ancients and the moderns that divides into three parallel histories and concludes with a long epilogue, in which she looks back on this now completed story to reflect on the end of European drama and European philosophy. The premise of her essay is simple but powerful: of all the literary genres from the epic to lyric poetry, from drama to the novel, from chronicles of the kings to historiography two alone are unique to Europe. They are tragedy and philosophy, the crowning creations of the Athenian polis. Just as philosophy must be distinguished from the wisdom literature common to all the world's civilizations, so tragedy must be distinguished from the theatre and drama of the world. Unlike comic phenomena and comedy, tragedy is not an anthropological universal. It appears only under certain specific conditions, of which the most important is the clash between old and new worlds, old and new values. In Athens it involved the passage from the old tribal clan structure to the new civic structure of the polis. In London and Paris, it involved the consolidation of the centralized power of the monarchy and the birth of modernity. The elective affinity which Heller means when she speaks of a parallel history is that between tragic drama and metaphysical philosophy. This affinity is the key to the first two of the parallel histories that she presents.

The first is the short epoch, some fifty years, of the great tragedies from Aeschylus to Euripides, followed by the equally short period from Plato to Aristotle. Here the historical sequence is crucial: the birth of philosophy goes together with the death of tragedy. If Heller reads this sequence as a crime as Nietzsche famously did in *The Birth of Tragedy from the Spirit of Music* she sees it at the same time as the unfolding of two stages of the one process of reflection on the relation between men and gods, ethics and destiny.

The second is the rebirth of tragedy in late Elizabethan England and then in France, covering some ninety years from Marlowe's *Tamerlane* to Racine's *Phaedra*. This rebirth of tragedy is the prelude to the two hundred years of European metaphysical systems from Descartes to Hegel. This second parallel history is not as straightforward as the first in that it stands between the ancients and the moderns. The long-fought quarrel between the ancients and the moderns was triggered by Corneille's *The Cid* in 1637. Corneille had already translated Aristotle's *Poetics* and now he was forced to rewrite his 'tragicomedy' to conform to the classical model of tragedy with its three unities of space, time, and plot. In turn, as with the ancients, tragedy preceded the renewal of metaphysics. There was at the same time, however, another, directly parallel history of drama and philosophy that extends from the presence of Machiavelli and Montaigne in Shakespeare to the Cartesian rationalism of Corneille's dialogues to Racine's Jansenist education and sympathies and the centrality of the rational-irrational duality of the passions (Pascal's 'reasons of the heart') in his protagonists, analysed by Heller in *Phaedra*.

The third epoch of the parallel history takes us from the ancients to the moderns. On the one hand it overlaps with the completion of metaphysics in Kant and Hegel and the search in classical German drama for a self-reflective renewal of tragedy (Schiller, Goethe, Hölderlin) that ends in what Heller calls the empty 'will to tragedy' in the plays of Hebbel. On the other hand, this third epoch takes off from Diderot's search in the 1750s for a post-tragic drama, that is, 'serious drama,' suited to the rising bourgeoisie that found its contemporary exemplification in Lessing's dramas of domestic life centred on the place and fate of women. The new drama after Racine is post-tragic just as philosophy after Hegel is post-metaphysical. It is post-tragic because it no longer revolves around the tragic clash between old and new values but around competing values in the one, shared 'modern condition.' But whether we speak of drama or philosophy, both stand under the sign of Hegel's dictum on the end of history and its inbuilt irony of the triumph of historicism in the 19th century's grand narratives of progress or decline.

Drama and philosophy after Hegel, after the watershed of the French Revolution, are each confronted by the question of their own possibility. They thus share a common discursive space evident in the response of dramatists from Büchner in the 1830s to Brecht in the 1930s to the challenges of historical change and of the radical philosophers from Schopenhauer and Feuerbach, Marx and Kierkegaard to Nietzsche and Freud, each with his own version of the end of history. Their ideological impact up to the Second World War and beyond forms the backdrop to the readings of the music dramas of Wagner and the plays of Ibsen, Chekhov, Strindberg, the Naturalists Hauptmann and Gorky, through to Shaw, Brecht and Sartre. And here with Sartre at the end of the Second World War we may say that the history of European drama has reached the limit of its possibilities. Is this also the case for philosophy in the 20th century? Not quite, the endgame of drama in the 1950s – Beckett's and Ionesco's tragicomedies and comedies of the absurd – anticipates the in/conclusion of the endgame of European philosophy in Derrida's endless interpretations.

3 Agnes Heller's Commitment to the Future

Where does this leave Agnes Heller herself? What part does she play in her story? The fourth and last part of her parallel history of drama and philosophy is the key here. This epilogue spells out what she announces at the very beginning of her essay in retrospection: stories can only be told once they are completed. The end of the story is the highest standpoint possible for the task of interpretation, that is, for the giving of meaning. Here she follows Hegel and ratifies his understanding of modernity as the realization and hence end of History and of Absolute Spirit in the truth, the prosaic truth, of accomplished modernity as the instituted embodiment of the idea of freedom. Hegel's arrival in European modernity becomes for Heller in the 21st century the arrival in global modernity that signifies the end of modern European history and its grand narrative of progress as well as the end of European art, religion and philosophy as a now completed history, in which the moderns are already on the way to becoming the ancients of global modernity. This leaves, however, the question of the European idea and institutions of freedom and their future open because freedom for Heller is paramount among modernity's three logics (capitalism, science, democracy) without which modernity can neither survive nor prosper.

This last part of the parallel history is Agnes Heller's testament, in which she takes her farewell from the greatness of the whole European history of tragedy and metaphysics, drama and philosophy. In relation to Europe and its Absolute Spirit she is a Hegelian but in relation to the idea and institutions of freedom she is a Kantian. The end does not denote nostalgia for what has passed nor does it rehearse a culturally pessimistic narrative of decline and fall. On the contrary Agnes Heller's farewell is close to Beckett's comic spirit that shines through the vain endgame of waiting for Godot, the Messiah to come. The story of Europe reached its completion in the generalization of modernity. This is the view from the end, the highest standpoint available and it encompasses Heller's own farewell to philosophy. She places her writings since *A Philosophy of History in Fragments* in the last of what she sees as the four central themes of philosophy in the 20th century, ranging from the reform or re-foundation of epistemology to the overcoming of metaphysics through the return to origins, and from the search for a new discourse theory to reflections on the task of philosophy. Hermeneutic reflection, as distinct from epistemological or metaphysical concerns, involves precisely reflection on the end of philosophy in the form of interpretations in relation to the philosophical tradition or in relation to art, the sciences, religion and political institutions. This process of reflection expresses for Heller the spirit of our times now that there is nothing essentially new to say.

As indicated, there is one crucial exception. The struggle for and the contestation of freedom unite the beginning of the story of Europe in Athens and its end in its legacy of freedom that defines the real and enduring battlefield of a generalized modernity. In this struggle philosophy becomes critique, that is, the expression of the challenge and necessity to think for oneself. If Europe's past survives in the memory of tragedy and thinks itself in the history of philosophy, Europe's present lives in the affirmation of the spirit of freedom. Hermeneutics as practised by Heller is thus a personal commitment as much to the past of the present as to the future of the present. The position at the end of the story is, she knows, that of the rear guard but it is not a position of despair or resignation but of perennial hope.

However, such an 'end of history' or 'Goodbye to philosophy' has to be rightly understood. In one of her earlier essays she made the point that Habermas's idea of the 'imperfect Enlightenment' is a never realised goal because all ideals are incomplete and imperfect. We are faced with the present as a challenge to meet to the remaining and new imperfections by asserting our practical freedoms. This awareness allows us to avoid the presumption that an 'end of history' implies a process of inevitable decline with nothing new. The complex multi-dimensional logics of modern societies have realised universal progress as an ideal endorsed around the globe, despite its many empirical breaches and shortfalls. These are the contradictions and tensions that can always be faced. A realised idea of freedom was a product of this long history of tragic drama and philosophy. It produced the normative ideals that have been universalised across of the world. These ideals have even allowed the realisation of this programme to be emphatically critiqued from the post-colonial perspective of those systematically excluded by race, religion, sexuality and gender. Heller concludes that one can only really talk about the "end of history" if one can be sufficiently confident that one knows what comes next. This is a position that can never be attained. The most difficult task is always before us. To the end the spirit of Agnes Heller is optimism while, at the same time, conceding that Utopia is beyond our reach and that we are hemmed in on all sides. Yet we still have the freedom and practical capacities to move forward.

PART 1

Tragedy and Philosophy

1   What Do Tragedy and Philosophy Have in Common?

In his preface to the *Philosophy of Right,* Hegel remarked that as the owl of Minerva begins to fly when darkness has set in, philosophy flourishes when a history comes to its end. One always understands history from its end. The endpoint is the starting point of reconstruction and of understanding the whole. Our age, Hegel believed, is the consummation and the end of history. This is why philosophy is able to reconstruct and understand history, including its own.

In the spring and summer of a historical age, poetry, and especially tragedy, dominates the scene. It happened in Athens, it happened again in modern Europe. Just when tragedy came to an end in the works of Euripides, philosophy was given birth by Socrates and flourished until it ended in Aristotle. The same happened in European history. As modern tragedy from Shakespeare to Racine left the scene, philosophy began its flight with Descartes to finally arrive at its end in Hegel. The end of tragedy was once again the prelude to the story of philosophy from the beginning to its end.

The question remains whether Hegel's remark offers a solid stepping-stone for further inquiries or whether it should be dismissed as one of Hegel's witty *apercus*? Let me assume that Hegel made a good point and take his *apercu* as a fitting conception, even if just as a hypothesis. First, I have to presume that there is something in common between tragedy and philosophy. The latter appears when the former disappears, as if philosophy carried a similar message to tragedy while in a way replacing it. Before beginning my inquiry, I have to make clear that I speak in the following both of tragedy and philosophy as literary genres. I do not ask the question whether one can speak of 'tragedies of life' or of 'tragic events' and I do not include in my inquiry the so-called moralists.

Aristotle in his *Poetics* already detected an important similarity between tragedy and philosophy. Both of them confront the spectator or the reader with something essential about the world: stories of men and gods, human ethics and destiny, the universe and destiny in general. Both of them, adds Aristotle, differ from history writing, since historians tell us how certain things happened or what certain things are, whereas philosophers and tragic writers do something else. They tell us how things might have happened, how they might have been, how they should be – by probability or by necessity. In history books contingencies play an important role, but in tragedy and philosophy the contingencies are subjected to or inserted into destiny or necessity.

Aristotle's observation as to what should have happened, should or might have been applies equally to philosophy and to tragedy. Yet what happens in a tragedy unfolds in a plot, whereas what happens in a philosophy unfolds in arguments and demonstration. Both stories and arguments lead equally to the final result and both are teleologically constructed. Aristotle presupposed that good tragedy writers know the end of their story before they begin. He suggested further that this result should be final. He disapproved of tragic series. Where something ends it should end with nothing else to begin. This is why most tragedies need to end with death. Not because death is in itself tragic, but because it is final. Tragedies are closed worlds, as are traditional (metaphysical) philosophies. The philosopher knows the outcome of his arguments or his demonstration before he begins them. He knows what the supreme Good or the supreme Truth is before he begins the deduction and arrives at its conclusion.

True, the three unities in tragedy (of time, action and place) suggested by Aristotle do not apply to philosophy. Yet it turned out that the unity of place and time does not apply to tragedy either. However, the unity of action does apply to both. The world presented by philosophers is supposed to be coherent, free of self-contradictions and finite. Nevertheless, they never succeed in the eyes of the next philosopher. The unity of time (and perhaps of place) is required according to Aristotle in a tragedy and in drama in general for reasons of transparency, in order that the audience retain the action as a whole in memory. One can quote one or the other episode from Homer without reference to the whole. In tragedy – and in philosophy – there are no episodes independent of the whole. In philosophy one has to have the *archai* (the principles) and the end result (the truth) simultaneously in mind to understand. On the contrary, one can understand one chapter in a history book, for example, the story of a war or the character of a king, without needing to have in mind the whole story.

Both philosophy and tragedy are literary genres. They both operate with characters. The characters in philosophy are called categories. Philosophers create their own stories by moving those characters as puppets in their world theatre. There are stock characters in philosophy such as substance, truth, reason, opinion, soul, principle and the like. Philosophers play with these characters on the world stage. They all create a world of their own, mostly with the same characters, yet in several variations. Their world is a closed one where everything is related to everything else, a consistent world, just like the world of tragedy. The end is final. True, all 'final' systems in philosophy are rejected by the next philosopher, who plays a different game with the same or similar characters.

Tragedies, however, are independent 'atoms,' they do not refer to one another either in affirmative or in negative terms. In addition, the anthropological roots of tragedy and philosophy are essentially different. One difference is obvious. Tragedy is, according to Aristotle, a sub-genre within the general genre of art (*techné*). *Techné* is mimesis, that is, imitation of sorts. According to Aristotle, imitation of nature. The concept of *techné* includes not just poetry or drama or painting but also the tools of practical use. Aristotle emphasizes the obvious: from early childhood we always imitate. We cannot grow up without imitating.

We are all thrown by accident as strangers into an alien world. Our genetic endowments have to assimilate, up to a degree, the world into which we were thrown. We have to learn the language, the use of things, the customs and the dominating world interpretations of the world into which we have been thrown. Without the capacity of imitation (mimesis) none of us could survive. *Techné* thus mobilizes one of the fundamental human conditions. Tragedy as a drama, according to Aristotle, 'imitates' nature by imitating actions. The main actions in all dramas are speech acts. Drama develops in dialogues and in speech acts. Similarly, actions in philosophy develop in speech acts. With the possible exception of Plato's Socratic dialogues (mentioned by Aristotle) speech acts in philosophy are the actions proper and they stand for themselves, whereas in drama speech acts represent, introduce, or reflect upon actions of life, actions of bodies including mute actions. One does not kill or die in speech, neither does one walk away, flee, crown oneself, marry, sail or blind oneself only in speech. But in philosophy everything is done by speech, that is, in concepts. The referents are also concepts.

Aristotle distinguishes tragedy and comedy mainly by the social and personal standing of the characters. The protagonists of a tragedy stand higher than us, the spectators, they are greater, nobler, whereas the characters of a comedy stand lower than us, they are vulgar, ugly or, in the worse instance, just like us. It is an open case whether by 'high' Aristotle meant high in rank (gods, kings or queens, princes, princesses) or high in personal importance, in moral nobility, since we cannot ask him. On the one hand, Aristotle emphasized that characters are less important than the plot and suggested that the poet first chooses the conflict, and only then looks for mythological figures which might be fitted best into the invented role. The characters should fit the plot and not vice versa. Tragic characters, formidable characters, great in stature, Aristotle continues, should make a serious mistake that will be the cause of their doom.

This mistake, he adds, should be rooted in their character (like the inclination to rage or irrational belief or disbelief) but it cannot result from evil intention. Doom by evil intention does not awake our empathy and doom without mistakes is sad but not tragic.

In his well-known novel *The Name of the Rose* set in the Middle Ages, Umberto Eco makes us believe that Aristotle's lost treatise on comedy might have had great significance for readers of that time and of our own. This belief fitted the plot of good fiction, yet, knowing Aristotle, one cannot think that the lost treatise had the same merit as the one on tragedies. For a very simple reason: the great Greek tragedies had already been written by Aristotle's time, no essential and significant tragedy was created after his time in the ancient world. As far as comedy is concerned, Aristotle knew only Aristophanes as *the* comic drama writer. He did not know the Greek 'new comedy,' an entirely new type of comedy, continued with success by great Roman comedy writers like Plautus and Terence. In their comedies, human characters could be also noble and wise. This new comedy opened a new path for comic drama. It is less satirical, less political than the comedies of Aristophanes. It is also far more mimetic, imitating comic scenes, speeches, vices in 'nature,' that is, in common human life. Certain typical tragic events in Greek tragedy, such as the reversal of fate or the recognition scene, from this period onwards will characterize comic rather than tragic drama (see Moliere or Mozart).

I introduced the philosophy of tragedy with a brief visit to Aristotle's *Poetics* because Aristotle was the first to offer a theory of drama in general and of tragedy in particular. He remained for many centuries the philosophical authority in matters of art and especially of tragedy. Plato, however, was the first philosopher to address the issue of poetics theoretically. One of Aristotle's major categories, 'mimesis,' had already been discussed by Plato.

Aristotle's work is polemical, and his polemic is directed essentially against Plato. However, the reader does not notice his polemical intention, since Aristotle's style (in contrast to Plato's) is rather a kind of balanced argumentative prose. Plato's polemical intent centres mainly around the relation between tragedy and philosophy and around the moral effect of poetry in general. The two problems are intimately related to the difference between Plato's and Aristotle's ethics and politics.

I mentioned Aristotle's suggestion that imitation of nature is the common feature of all arts and that imitation is, as it indeed is, an anthropological universal. Mimesis belongs to human life. Yet, for Plato mimesis is suspect, suspect ontologically and morally alike. Ontologically, as he states in *The Republic,* because the empirical world is itself an imitation, a shadow of the reality (truth) of the world of ideas. Ontologically philosophy and poetry occupy two extreme positions of the continuum. Philosophy leads people from the empirical world up to the real and true one, from darkness to the light. Poetry, in contrast, imitates the world of shadows, and as such it is the shadow of the shadow.

Where morality is concerned, mimesis can be accepted, according to Plato, only if a work imitates the deeds of good men, who are rewarded for their goodness. Homer lies about the gods and this makes him therefore morally and politically dangerous. Only certain passages of his work should be available to be read or recited in the ideal city state. How can it be allowed that a man who murdered his father and married his mother be presented as the hero of a drama? Plato introduces additional arguments to his moral charges against drama. A virtuous person, he argues, always says what he thinks. What about the actor? He has to present other persons, not himself. He has to say things alien to his own convictions. He is a chameleon, one person one day and another person the next. At the end, he does not know what he is or who he is. All the three objections against 'mimetic art' will be repeated later on in the story of the family conflicts between philosophy and tragedy.

Let me end with a brief discussion about philosophy's relation to tragedy and return to a question mentioned earlier but not yet followed up. This is the question concerning the difference between the anthropological roots of tragedy and comedy. Besides both being drama and mimetic art, are they also in addition manifestations and expressions of the same anthropological universal? As a starting point, I will refer only to the one of their anthropological differences that will be decisive in their future development and history.

Let me begin again at the beginning: the accident of birth. We all are thrown into a particular world by accident. There is nothing in our genetic endowment that fits us to this world rather than any other human world, into any place or into any time. In order to survive every human has to learn to fit into the particular human world, where he or she has been born. The new-born is an absolute unique being and also an absolute universal being (a *homo sapiens* with unique genetic endowment). The mediation between the singular and the universal is 'outside' and one needs to internalize it by externalizing oneself actively.

This manoeuvre normally succeeds, yet mostly not completely. There always remains a gap between the unique persons and the world into which they were thrown. They will never completely fit. This gap is the cause of discontent in civilizations in general, not just in one or other civilization. *Civilization and its Discontents* as Freud called it. Without constant discontent there would never be any changes: that is civilization.

There are two omnipresent reactions to this gap and to their expression: laughter and crying. Both laughter and crying are anthropological universals as they are present in all human worlds. If one takes the position of the *social* a priori, one begins to laugh. This is why laughter is social: we all laugh together. If we take the position of our *genetic* a priori, pity ourselves and feel for ourselves, we are crying; we cry in solitude. Comic dramas make us laugh, just as we laugh on many other occasions. The comic phenomenon is everywhere: starting with comic imitations, parodies, caricatures, continuing with comic genres like comic novels, paintings, jokes and comic performances, those of clowns, comedians and practical jokers. No question then that comic drama is rooted in an anthropological universal.

What about tragedies? Are they manifestations of anthropological universal crying or are they expressions of another tragic universal experience? Is death tragic? Is tragic experience a form of self-identification rooted in self-pity? It is easy to see that the opposite is the case. At this point, again, Aristotle was the genius who invented the obvious. The audience, the recipient of a tragedy, experiences *catharsis*. What is *catharsis*? It is the liberation from our own fears and self-pity and the 'purification of our soul' from the identification with ourselves. This *catharsis* is due to our identification with the other not with ourselves. Is empathy not an anthropological universal? Surely it is, but it is not related to tragedy as a literary genre. One can also empathize with the happiness of others and with their deserved good fate. In mentioning empathy, let me return again for a moment to Aristotle's *Poetics*. His discussion of tragedy can also be perceived a critical answer to Plato's rejection of certain kinds of representation.

Plato was the first to speak of mimetic art. To repeat: tragedy is dangerous because it makes the public pity the heroes who do evil. They make them empathize with a man who killed his father and slept with his mother, According to Plato's *The Republic* (quoted with gusto by Freud) even good people dream sometimes of doing just the same but they are horrified by those dreams and they do not empathize with them. Aristotle's answer to this puzzle is simple. The spectators of the tragedy do not empathize with the crime but with the man who committed it unwittingly, who was deceived mostly, albeit not always, by a god. They empathize with a man who tried everything to avoid his fate and precisely by avoiding it fulfilled it. In sum, *catharsis* is not empathy but an emotional response to it. Aristotle also discusses the Oedipus case in his *Nicomachean Ethics* where he distinguishes between foreseeable and unforeseeable consequences of an action. No actor is morally responsible for the unforeseeable consequences of his deed. Oedipus is not guilty of patricide and incest. Yet Plato's position was also often accepted in modern times.

Both tragedy and comedy were often abused as politically and morally suspect genres and sometimes outlawed. Just like some philosophies.

Let me return to the question of universality. The comic phenomenon is seen as deeply seated in the human condition; comic genres make use of it, such as wit, jokes, satire, caricature, verbal duels, humour, 'uncivilized' use of bodily parts, and outwitting others. Comic phenomena are present everywhere and empirically universal, even if comic drama, born in Athens, that makes use of them all, is not. Are there tragic phenomena that are not as universal as comic ones? It depends on what one calls tragic. Death is not tragic, since if it were, we would all be tragic heroes. Socrates in not a tragic hero and Christ was never regarded as tragic. Suffering is not tragedy. One speaks nowadays of tragic death when a young man is killed in a car accident or has committed suicide. One feels empathy for a fallen soldier or a betrayed lover without calling their fate tragic. What one calls a tragedy of life, as Plato already determined, does not refer to certain tragic subgenres (as in case of the comic) but to sad stories. We really empathize with sad stories, imagining ourselves in the place of those whose story we witnessed or read about. Our reactions can be different and not necessarily (even rarely) cathartic, ranging from empathy, crying, learning a lesson to malice.

To come to a preliminary conclusion: the two kinds of drama (comedy and tragedy) stand not just in different but also in opposite relations to anthropological universals. Tragedy liberates us from universals, while comedy manifests them. Based on this preliminary conclusion, one could already presuppose that the comic phenomenon is universal and present everywhere, whereas tragedy, since it does not embody or express a universal anthropological condition, does not provoke a universal answer to so-called tragic events and might only appear in very specific historical times and specific historical cultures.

Tragedy is a European genre that dominated the European scene only twice: in ancient Greece and in early modernity. Myths, these legends of polytheistic cultures, are to be found in all parts of the world and among all traditions. Myths cannot be tragic, given that gods are immortal: mythical stories appear in different shapes and they have different variations. Fairy tales are not tragic and not just because they normally have happy endings. Homer's great poems are not tragic as no *epos* is. Why are the biblical heroes not tragic? Why was there no tragedy in the Middle Ages? Why is monotheism unsuited to offer material for tragedy? One might first cast a glance at the main stories of the Jewish Bible. Some biblical characters (from Abraham through Samson to King David) are perfectly fitted to play the role of tragic heroes. They are men of grandeur who commit mistakes that reside in their characters. All conditions of a tragic plot described by Aristotle are met. Why then are they unsuited for becoming heroes of tragedies? I would say because the plots are essentially different from the mythological. The plots themselves are not tragic, even if they end with death as in the case of Samson. (See the discussion by George Steiner in his *Antigones* of Milton's *Samson Agonistes*.) Why not? Because the historical conditions are essentially different. The heroes of the biblical stories are participating in the chain of redemptive history. Their life and fate serve a divine purpose: they are saved by God and God is just and he never cheats like the Greek gods.

Greek and Roman gods interfere because there are many of them and they often act at cross purposes. Moreover, the ancient worlds have no future, *no telos*, but the Jewish and the Christian worlds are teleological, mediating between past and future, between the origin (creation) and the end, the *telos* (redemption, salvation, the second coming of Christ and the coming of the Messiah). The Almighty never cheats, never leads a character astray and even if his ways are not known, one thing can be known: that it is the way to salvation of a people or of a person. Medieval mystery plays cannot be tragic given that the end of life is the beginning of the hereafter or resurrection. Shakespeare's Hamlet is entirely conscious about the ontological conditions of tragedy. Ignorance about life after death (Hamlet's famous monologue) is one of its conditions. Baroque composers knew all about this difference, first and foremost Handel. Mythological figures and characters from Roman history play leading roles in his tragic operas, whereas biblical characters appear as the heroes of oratorios, including *Jephta* and *Saul*, even though their stories are clearly influenced by 'aboriginal' Greek myths.

What is the relation of philosophy to the human condition? Is there something in our anthropological make up one could identify as a universal human need for philosophy? Aristotle raises this question and seems to answer it. Every human being wants to know: these words introduce his 'first philosophy.' Yes, we all desire to know. Without getting to know the world into which we were thrown we would never be able to cope with this world and survive. We have to know something about the dominating world interpretation of our ancestors and contemporaries and be able to tell good from evil and right from wrong.

Every action or sentence has a meaning. But is there a meaning in the whole? In our life? Why is it *this* way and not another way? Why is there something rather than nothing? Such and similar questions and all the answers to these questions are partially based on everyday experience, partially on the dominating world interpretations (if there are several). Answers to these and similar questions, whether written down in prose or poetry or just orally mediated, satisfy the elementary need to know the world. Moreover, all high cultures we know about have wisdom literature, within or separate from religions that offer answers to those burning questions. There are some common features in all wisdom literatures that are due to the human condition shared in all cultural memories, and also some unique ones that are due to differences in cultural memory. There is a particularly significant literature of wisdom in India, China, in the Bible, in Persia and certainly also in Greece. Yet, although their function is similar, they are not philosophies.

This is why the word 'philosophy' was coined by Socrates for the very purpose to distinguish it as 'love of wisdom' (*philo/sophos*) from the real or presumed authors of wisdom literature (*sophos*). Most of the so-called pre–Socratic philosophers, like the first Ionian ones, as far as we know them from their fragments, were authors of wisdom literature. They became included in the history of philosophy because Plato regarded them as his predecessors and quoted them. Wisdom literature stands neither lower nor higher than philosophy but is simply different. One conclusion can already be drawn: neither tragedy nor philosophy is rooted in the anthropological (human) condition, or if they are, they are just one of the expressions or manifestations of our innate desire to know. The Athenian genius created two new literary genres: tragedy and philosophy. They are European genres. They were born in Europe, flourished in Europe and finally died there.

Whenever a genre is established, one can step into it, keeping it alive by offering continuity. Something similar happened to the *epos*. Epic poetry was as widespread as wisdom literature in times of the origin of a people. We know great epic poems from India, Persia, Greece and Iceland. Virgil already stepped into the tradition and there were several retrospective attempts to discover the epics of the new people entering Europe with the great migrations. The romantic belief that only an epos about the origin makes a people great caught the imagination. I know only of one successful attempt at revival: Wagner's music drama, *The Ring*. Still, the epic genre died out, because not only its ontological but also its ideological foundation had gone.

Let me run a little ahead. Tragic drama in the ancient understanding of tragedy was beginning to die at the time when the novel became the dominating literary genre. Still, there remained many writers who stepped into the tragic drama tradition. They wrote sad plays ending with death. The Germans termed these plays *bürgerliche Trauerspiele* (bourgeois tragedies), the French 'serious drama' to distinguish them from proper tragedies. Serious dramas and tragicomedies were finally replaced in the second part of the 20th century with absurd drama. What remains today is the 'play,' theatres are flourishing, new plays need to be written and to be performed. This marks the final end of tragedy. And what happened with philosophy? Hegel was right. Metaphysics as philosophy ended together with its claim to totality. Whether European philosophy altogether ended with metaphysics remains to be seen.

True, philosophy flourished in Europe, yet only in certain times and in certain places, and it never dwelled in the same place continuously for a long time. Since philosophy is not dependent on ontological conditions, its 'homes' are not continuous in time, even less in place. Philosophy, like tragedy, is a bird of passage, yet it built nests in more times and more places than tragedy. Invented in Athens as a metaphysical system, it was absorbed by the learned stratum in imperial Rome as guidance to a good life. After centuries of intermission it returned again as metaphysical systems in the Middle Ages in Southern and in Western Europe, with God as the Supreme Being, as Truth, as the pinnacle of the system.

Modern philosophy set roots roughly in the same places as ancient and the medieval philosophy, while it began slowly to emigrate (to fly) during the Renaissance from Italy to France and Britain and only later to Germany. There was no original philosophy in any other European state or nation. There was one single Spinoza in Holland (he was Jewish), one Kierkegaard in Denmark (immersed in the Bible and schooled by German philosophy). One could add that even after the collapse of the metaphysical system, that is, after Hegel, significant philosophers emerged exactly from the same soils. One could come up with the hypothesis that original philosophies appeared in times of significant social transformations of the dominant world explanation. Something similar now happened to philosophy as had already happened with tragedy. After the collapse of the Hegelian system, several representative thinkers stepped into the tradition of the philosophical literary genre.

Even before Hegel not all philosophers were system builders, but after him, there is no system builder with any kind of significance. What remained of traditional philosophical thinking is the division of the empirical and the transcendental level of inquiry, and hermeneutics as the interpretation of the other (art, science, history, religion, politics, institutions in general). It leads sometimes to the blurring of difference between philosophy and its *interpretandum,* given that hermeneutics is practiced on quite different texts or institutions as texts. Just as tragedy was replaced by serious dramas, tragicomedy and finally by absurd drama, so the holistic transparent philosophical systems were replaced by philosophical fragments. Are they really parallel stories?

2   Tragedy: Its Conditions and Constituents

Tragedy appears in times when a world is not just changing, but when two essentially different worlds – the old and new – are clashing, while this clash manifests itself in human conflicts where there is right and wrong on both sides. In modern tragedies (but not necessarily in the Greek) the clash of the two worlds manifests itself not just externally, that is, in actions, but also internally, within the mind and the soul of the protagonists. Let us cast a glance on the way tragic writers do what they do. One can rely upon Hegel in his lectures on *Aesthetics* since he could also take modern tragedy into consideration. Tragedy is drama. There are three necessary constituents of a drama: the general state of the world, the situation and finally the action. Yet, they are different in tragedy and comedy.

Let me begin with the general state of the world. Shakespeare, who was not just the greatest modern tragic writer but also the most reliable theorist of tragedy, formulated precisely the state of the world in tragedies: 'the time is out of joint.' A 'time out of joint' is the first and necessary condition of tragedy. In both times when immortal tragedies were born, times were out of joint. They were the times where the old world collapsed and a new world was born or about to be born. This general state of the world is a necessary condition for the birth of tragedy, yet not the sufficient condition for its rebirth.

Hegel distinguishes the state of the world and the situation. What kind of situation? A situation where the old and the new stand directly on a collision course, both represented by characters who fight out the collision, and where the worlds also collide in one of the main characters' soul. Whereas for Aristotle the backbone of a tragedy was the plot, for Hegel it is 'the proper character in the proper situation.'

Tragedy is also dependent upon the needs, the expectation, the possible – not actual – life experience of a theatre audience. It stands to reason that the most significant tragedies were born in cities. In fact, in three cities: Athens, London, and Paris. Yet, their plots were rarely set in the same city and also rarely in the present time. Since tragedy is played on the stage for a few hours, it develops on the stage (even if we later read them). It is always taking place in the present, developing before our eyes, even though the end remains hidden until the last scene, even if we already know the story.

I said repeatedly Athens, although I speak often of Greek tragedy. Among all the Greek city states, only Athens created tragedy. Still, there is good a reason to speak of Greek tragedy, since the cult of theatre, of tragic and comic drama, became the typical identity mark of Greek influence and cultural domination. Hellenistic and Roman cities were proud of their theatres. Roman tragedies,

Seneca's dramas included, unlike Roman comedies were far inferior and far more cruel and bloody variations on Greek themes. Still, the cult of gladiators did not entirely overshadow the cult of theatre actors even in Rome.

Why I said London is obvious. The Elizabethan theatre was and remains the peak period of modern tragedy, as Shakespeare was and remains by far the greatest modern writer of tragedy. Why I said Paris is perhaps less obvious. For a century Corneille and Racine were regarded as the great modern tragic poets and were even placed above Shakespeare. Even if their tragedies are rarely played nowadays outside of France, one has to presuppose that they made certain conflicts manifest before they were addressed by mainstream philosophy. To speak about the end of tragedy is less simple than to associate tragedy with the above mentioned three cities.

In modern times, the strict division between the tragic and comic poet became outdated. Socrates in Plato's *Symposium* suggested that the poet should write tragedy and comedy, obviously referring to his own philosophical dialogues as both tragic and comic. Yet the first poet, who wrote both tragedies and comedies and in addition 'romances,' was Shakespeare. He also did something unheard of: there were comic scenes in his tragedies and tragic scenes in his comedies. Some of the greatest French poets tried to excel in both genres. However, a tragedy by Moliere or a comedy by Corneille is far below the artistic level of their chosen genres. In order to not pour water into the ocean of expertise, I will just make a case for my parallel history.

We know the empirical history of the birth of ancient tragedy from Aristotle. First came the theatre, the public presentation of poetry as choral song, the dithyramb invented for and practiced on the occasion of the Dionysian mysteries. The chorus occupied the scene, as mythological stories and lyrics were used in the cult of this alien deity. Then one actor was placed beside the chorus, followed by two actors and then by three. From this the dramatic genres of tragedy and comedy were born. Whether the actors sang or spoke remains up for discussion. That the chorus was singing we know from Aristotle, yet he does not make mention of singing actors. It may be assumed that they presented their poetic verse following the rhythm of the meter in a declamatory manner. French classic tragedies are still played in the *Comédie Francaise* in this way and so was Shakespeare in my youth in the National Theatre in Budapest. (I confess that I like the declamatory presentation better than a Hamlet and Ophelia talking to each other as if they were sitting in a corner café.)

According to Hegel, goals and purposes are individualized in all tragedies. An individual needs to be free in order to set his or her own goals. This means that the *telos*, the end or the outcome develops from the internal to the external, from the soul/mind to the deed. The action is not just an answer to a stimulus but the manifestation of the actor's character. The situation of an action is not simply something pre-existing, it is created and realizes the situation exactly of this or that character. Whoever acts in a situation creates the situation. His or her pathos moves and motivates the actor, and this pathos is nothing but the universal spirit, that is, everything essentially of value for the actor, such as family, country and honour. An individual acts by being mobilized by his or her pathos, and is crossed by another individual mobilized by an alternative pathos. These two *pathé* (passions) collide. This is the fate or rather the destiny of all tragic actors.

It is interesting to note that Hegel does not distinguish between the ancient Greek concept of fate echoed in Greek tragedies and the modern view of fate, formulated by Machiavelli and also by Shakespeare. In the first case destiny is activated by a man's deed, in the second case, it is created by him. Hegel differentiates subjective and objective pathos. The pathos of a lyric poet can be subjective, yet the pathos of a tragic actor needs to be both objective and subjective. Interest alone should not motivate the tragic hero, not even a personified general interest. The tragic situation and conflicts are characterized by the totality of the action and not by the totality of ideas or things.

The tragic collision, this either/or, is the pinnacle in the tragic drama. The fundamental conflict ends with reconciliation of the colliding ethical and spiritual powers. Hegel reinterprets Aristotle's theory of catharsis in this spirit. Aristotle could not have meant that the audience finds relief through emotions like fear and pity; he must have meant the reconciliation of two colliding spiritual powers. Tragedies should end with the reconciliation of the two clashing powers where both sides have put their life at stake. Here Hegel applies the idea of putting life at stake from his *Phenomenology* (the chapter on 'Master and Slave') as well as the concept of *Versöhnung* (reconciliation) from his *Elements of a Philosophy of Right*. Tragedy, according to Hegel, ends with the reconciliation of two colliding universal powers, of the objective and the subjective spirit, the reconciliation of reason and actuality. Similarly, in Hegel's system, the philosophy of Absolute Spirit ends with the reconciliation of method and system. Again, a kind of brotherhood between tragedy and philosophy as it was suggested in quite a different way in Aristotle's *Poetics*.

All significant theorists or philosophers of art over generalise. Philosophy of art, in our case philosophy of tragedy, is a case of hetero-interpretation. Philosophy interprets or understands not another philosophy but another literary genre. This approach is always a hermeneutical exercise, in our case a double hermeneutical exercise. One can try to mediate another philosophy with one's own, but also another literary genre (in our case tragedy) with the world and also with the philosophy of one's own time. Gadamer suggests that the aim should be the fusion of the two horizons. This might be the aim. However, it will be never achieved. Or if one supposes that it can, as Hegel and Nietzsche sometimes did, or at least that it should, we children of the 21st century do not share this belief. We presume that everyone has to read the tragedies again and again and that this will be another tragedy with every new reading.

Tragedy has three conditions and five constituents. The three conditions are shared by comedies as well, whereas the five constituents are not. The three conditions are theatre, work and audience. Theatre is an institution, mostly also a building, serving as a home, as the place to present a play for an audience. Tragedy was born as part of the Dionysian festivities in Greece, even though Dionysus was a stranger in Greece, an alien Asian god, although presumably the son of Zeus and a Semele. Yet, even if the cult (the cultic songs included) was not a Greek invention, the introduction of an actor first enabled the collision of purposes, emphasized by Hegel, to develop. First one, then two, then three actors (Sophocles) were added to the choral song and a new literary genre was born. Amphitheatres were built for the purpose of staging dramas. In the age of Hellenism amphitheatres were built wherever Greek was spoken. But while theatres were mushrooming, no significant tragedies were written, just the great 'ancients' were re-staged.

In the Roman Republic the public places served religious-patriotic purposes and were used also for games, yet theatre was entirely unknown until the last two centuries of the Republic. Tragedy arrived with Greek culture, with the foreign taste and growing cultivation of Greek language and literature. In imperial times drama performances became popular. Roman playwrights wrote innovative comedies. In fact, Plautus and Terence established the tradition of modern comic drama without contributing to the world of tragedy. Seneca tried, without matching the Greeks.

Ancient dramatists were highly honoured citizens of the city. Drama competitions took place each year at the time of Dionysian festivities. Winners of the drama competition were as famous as the winners of the Olympic games. In Athens public topics were addressed to public audiences both in tragic drama (which normally consisted of three parts and a satyr play) and in comic drama (Aristophanes). Comic drama later took the form of the new Greek and Roman comedies where the plot became private, as it remained mostly thereafter. That a private plot can also be political was already known in ancient times.

Up to the 18th century there was no drama without theatre and without an audience. The audience could be wider or narrower. Whether in a city theatre or in a court theatre, spectators were sitting in a theatre. Plays were also performed in castles and noble homes as private performances for family and friends. Sometimes roles were learned and played by the members of the family and neighbours. Only from the 19th century onwards did it become a habit to read tragedies just like novels, in one's bedroom or living room. Yet even then reading aloud, if only for a private audience, was preferred.

To repeat: the three conditions of the existence of tragic and comic drama are the same (theatre, work, audience). What I call existence is being known and cherished. Ancient Athenian dramas remained alive during the whole of antiquity; they and their now lost or inferior products were played before interested and involved audiences. For the same reason, they were not alive in the Middle Ages. There is no poetic existence without reception.

To return to one of the starting points: the constituents of the tragic and comic drama are different. The kind of 'universal state of the world' where certain characters in certain situations will meet a tragic fate that makes audiences experience empathy and fear is rare. It occurred only twice in European history, when a taken for granted and well-established world was suddenly shattered by a brand new world, when people no longer understood who they were and what was right and wrong, when old virtues collapsed and new virtues were born.

The first world-shattering experience I already mentioned. One can hardly imagine a deeper abyss than the one that divided tribal societies based on blood relations from city states based on the rule of laws, the 'natural' from the 'political.' Greek tragedies were the fruits of the collision of these two worlds, where both worlds were presented and represented by outstanding human characters. The models of these characters, their names and their stories were borrowed from Homer and Hesiod, from the world of the past, but their conflicts embodied in words and in actions expressed the present experiences of the writers. This dual character of tragedies, taking place in the past yet reflecting upon the present, remained a constant feature of the genre. Comedies not only develop in the present, they are also staging the present, whereas tragedies, unlike the owl of Minerva, stage a past resembling the present.

In Greek tragedy, the plot takes place in the mythological past that is overcome at the end (one exception to this is the historical play *The Persians*). Later in Shakespeare, the plot mainly takes place in the historical past, and not only the English history plays, but also in *Hamlet, Macbeth* or *King Lear*. French classic tragedy followed both heritages, as did baroque opera. From the Renaissance onwards the Greek tradition that combined the speech of dialogues and the songs of the chorus became divided and begun to develop separately as tragic drama on the one hand and on the other hand as musical drama. Tragic drama remained poetic (written in verse) yet was spoken. However, for a long time, tragedy preserved something of the musical character, thus declamation was the traditional and proper way to present it. The chorus in opera as in ancient tragedy is sung. The chorus reflects on the actions of the heroes and sometimes even intervenes, giving advice and formulating philosophical questions and moral judgments. This split between spoken and sung theatre sometimes even divided the audience. It also frequently led in musical theatre to the absolute domination of music, to the impoverishment of the operatic text and hence, as Wagner pointed out, to the loss of drama itself. The great exception was Da Ponte's libretti for Mozart's operas.

The main action in tragedies takes place in verbal conflicts, the *agon*. In Aeschylus and Sophocles, sometimes also in Euripides, two values, two passions and two worlds collide. There are hundreds of different modern interpretations of those values and of the passions they manifest. Some see in the *Oresteia* the conflict between matriarchy and patriarchy where the latter wins with Athena's vote, who was never a mother. In *Phenomenology of the Spirit* Hegel presents *Antigone* as the conflict between the laws of the gods and laws of the state. One can freely interpret these tragedies and one will never be able to understand what the authors really had in mind. And this is not even important.

From philosophers who interpreted the inscriptions of Delphi: 'nothing too much' and 'know thyself,' we can better understand what was at stake in the tragic *agon*. Modern thinkers often take side with one argument against the other, with one protagonist against the other. For example, for Goethe and Marx Aeschylus' Prometheus, who helped men and hated the gods, was a hero without blemish. Yet not so for the ancients since for them 'nothing too much' meant moderation in all things. As Aristotle knew: all tragic heroes commit mistakes due to a blemish in their character when they cross the line towards the extreme. We identify with *Antigone*. for she is the victim of a noble deed in burying her brother against the law, yet when she hates Ismene for her reluctance to follow her, even we, the latecomers, say 'too much.'

Although the plots of tragedies are taken from the past, they address their audience in the present. In Greek tragedies quite often the text becomes highly political, for example, a kind of *laudatio* to Athens and Athenian institutions. The *Oresteia* ends with a hymn of praise to Athena, the goddess of Athens and of the institution of the Areopagus, the new court of law, where the votes of the judges replace blood revenge. In Aeschylus' *The Suppliants,* the city offers haven for women who escape from forced marriages. It also testifies to the superiority of Athenian institutions that, before allowing strangers to stay, the king remarks that he cannot decide the issue alone and that he needs the vote of the people. At the end of the tragedy *Oedipus in Colonus* it is Theseus, the legendary founding father of Athens, who welcomes Oedipus, the dying stranger, to his city. The audience surely identified the dignified and just Theseus with the first citizen of Athens, Pericles.

Three common constituents of tragedy have been mentioned. The plot is taken from the past, although addressing the present, the work is written in verse and finally, the main action take place in the collision of worlds, the *agon*. The fourth common characteristic of tragedies and some comedies is the inclusion of philosophical-existential reflections. The action stands still while reflection takes its place. In Greek tragedy it is mainly the chorus who reflect on the actions and collisions philosophically-existentially, sometimes out of the blue. On other occasions, it is the main character. In Elizabethan tragedy, where there is no chorus, the function of existential reflection is taken over by the monologues. Here the main characters and sometimes common people hit the nail on the head.

The most famous philosophical chorus comes from Sophocles' *Antigone* and appears in an important context. A guard assigned to the corpse of Antigone's brother is accused by Creon of having buried Polynices' body himself or having helped others to do it against the law and for money. Creon cannot even imagine any motivations other than greed. Antigone appears and defends her deed after the song of the chorus. The famous chorus stands between these two scenes. It starts with the words: nothing is more *deinos* than men. Interpreters differ about the translation of *deinos*. What is man? *Deinos*. Humanists translate the word as 'wonderful,' anti-humanists (like Heidegger) as 'terrible.' The word, however, means both. In my view this is why the poet used it. 'Nothing is more wonderful/terrible than man.' The chorus continues with the enumeration of all the brilliant skills man developed by becoming the master of nature. It then turns to the capacity of speech and of thinking, and finally to the ability to create home (the state) and house. It is only death that man cannot escape.

Finally, in the last strophe the chorus of the old men unmask the duality of the word *deinos*. In using all their great achievements, 'man can turn them to evil as well as to the good.' Those who use these practices for the good are wonderful, those who use them for evil are terrible. Yet what happens if one cannot honour the laws of the state and the rights of the gods at the same time? Can Antigone or Creon be good? It turns out that Creon could have become good had he had the strength to honour the gods, allowing Antigone to do service to the god while making an exception to the law issued by himself. Antigone blindly follows her sisterly passions and since passion motivates her, she has no real choice. Here enters another motive that has nothing to do with the state, law and kingship. A man does not want to yield to a woman ('Never will women rule me in my life'). Tiresias the blind sage warns Creon and urges him to use his will. 'My son, come to your senses, every mortal can err in life.' However, Creon becomes more and more stubborn, listening to no one and accusing everyone including Tiresias of being bribed, finally causing his own doom.

Antigone contests a traditional understanding of ancient tragedy. According to this understanding, the centre of ancient tragedies was fate and destiny: that is, *moira* or *tyché*, whereas in modern tragedy everything depends on character. In my view, in Greek tragedy everything depended on the character and not on fate, only the belief in fate. The myth was reworked in the spirit of Athenian ethics. True, according to myth, the house of Thebes, born from dragon teeth, was cursed. Oedipus and his children were cursed, and they had to meet their fate. But Creon, also the son of the cursed Atrides, could have changed his mind at least three times. No *moira* made it impossible.

I have already arrived at the fifth constituent of all tragedies. Character decides the fate of all, characters keep tragedies in motion and lead them to the final outcome: to death. Death of the main character, death of several characters, death of a city and of a world. Sometimes, even often, the birth of a new world. *Antigone* is the third play of a trilogy: *Oedipus the King*, *Oedipus in Colonus*, and *Antigone*. *Oedipus in Colonus* was the last tragedy by the old Sophocles and it was not even performed in his lifetime. Some interpreters detect similarities between Euripides and this last play of Sophocles, rightly in my judgment. I do not suggest direct influence, although on receiving the news of Sophocles' death, Euripides made the actors in the performance of his tragedy appear in mourning. One should bear in mind the changed times, the great period of Athenian democracy and the blossoming of dramatic poetry, between the victory over the Persians until the Peloponnesian war, lasted no longer than half a century. Sophocles died old. He saw it all. Still, whereas Sophocles remained to the end the faithful son of Athens, and the poet of Athens' grandeur, Euripides, at least according to Aristotle, was not a good citizen. In fact, he escaped to Macedonia.

After having mentioned the fourth and the fifth constituents of tragedy: philosophical-existential reflection and the presentation of character as the moving power of all tragedies, ancient and modern, I will briefly exemplify them by the two inscriptions of Delphi.

In the mythological stories of Oedipus and his family, destiny, fate, not free volition, decided both the development and the end. Because tragic authors borrowed the plot roughly but not entirely from the mythological tradition, they had to remain true to it. Yet, remaining roughly true to the plot did not mean acceptance of the message. Apollo saw the future. Yet, that someone, Apollo or even Cassandra, saw the future did not mean that they determined the future.

Let me give a Christian example. God is omniscient and eternal (not temporal like the Greek gods). For Him there is no difference between past, present and future. Therefore, He knows the future. But this does not mean that He determines the actions of actors of that future. Almost the same can be said about ancient tragedy. Look at the fate of Oedipus. His father Laios was told that if he has a son his son will murder him and marry his wife Jocasta. This is why they abandoned the baby child. Laios and Jocasta decided this, not the gods. They did the wrong thing. This is exactly how the dying Oedipus sees it. *Oedipu*s arrives at Colonus as a stranger, as he also arrived as a stranger to Thebes, asking for haven in the sanctuary of the Eumenides, the former Furies and torturers of Orestes, who were pacified by Athena, as we know from the *Oresteia*. Oedipus is accompanied by his daughters Antigone and Ismene. It is here that *Oedipus* reflects upon his history and what he did and why, on his guilt or innocence, very much in the spirit of the ethical ideas in Sophocles' time.

Guilty or not guilty? Guilty of what? Did his guilty acts follow from his character? Or were they somehow determined? For what is Oedipus morally responsible? Why am I the evil one? This is the question Oedipus puts in the dialogue with Creon, not in terms of the mythological tradition, but in terms of Aristotelian ethics. My father and my mother tried to kill me! Were they not guilty? Had I avenged myself on them wittingly, people would understand! Yet I did not know that I killed my father, I just killed a man in self-defence. Jocasta did not know that I was her son. On what moral ground am I guilty?

Here Oedipus raises the philosophical question as to whether someone is responsible for an act if he does not know what he is doing, neither the circumstances of his action nor the identity of the victims. No, he is not morally responsible for his evil deed and he is not evil. But is he responsible for nothing? 'What I did, I did freely, yet I did not will it' is his summary. He did not know he was killing his father, yet he killed a man. He said that he did it in self-defence. However, those who know his character (the whole audience then and since) cannot believe him. He is a man inclined to fits of rage, unjustly accusing people of bad motivations. Those who had seen *Oedipus the King* know it. Antigone knows it and finally Oedipus realizes it too. He now realizes that he blinded himself in a fit of rage. (His character reminds us of Othello, another stranger.) He is neither a patricide nor an innocent victim.

The race of dragon's teeth will die of their divine curse: their inherited uncompromising spirit, their constant anger and their constant *hubris*. As in the case of the famous choral ode in *Antigone*, the often-quoted pessimistic wisdom in '*Oedipus in Colonus*' also needs to be read in its context. Oedipus is old. The chorus of old men lament the suffering of old age. Then comes the often-quoted passage: 'The greatest happiness is never to be born' – verses written by an old man, who enjoyed the greatest gift a man can receive, earthy immortality, the gift of poetry, and even the respect, the adoration of his contemporaries.

And the end of the tragedy? The most beautiful death of a man called by a divine voice or taken by the earth, mourned by loving, caring daughters and respected by the great polis of the future: Athens. Only Theseus, the mythological founder of Athens, can see Oedipus' grave. One significant man, a noble man, a man of great suffering, a man inclined to extremes dies and a great city, Athens, is born. A kind of apotheosis. Perhaps it is not that unfortunate to be born, at least not in Athens. The dramatic verbal collisions in *Oedipus the King* already show deep insight into the then developing Athenian moral philosophy that goes far beyond the Ionian and Eleatic philosophies, the Delphi sanctuary and its oracle that advised Laios and Oedipus alike, and much later also Socrates, albeit ironically. The warnings 'nothing too much' or 'know thyself' were generally known and rarely obeyed.

As we know, Sophocles' Oedipus never obeyed this advice. For him nothing was too much, neither anger nor despair, neither justice nor injustice. And given his emotional character, did he take absolutely seriously that he should know himself, whatever the price. When he interrogates Tiresias and the shepherd about his origin, he is warned that it would be better for him and for everyone to remain ignorant. He says to Jocasta: 'I must see and know ... Come what comes ... I am the son of Destiny. My mother was Fate, my sisters and brothers the mouths with whom I grew.' 'I am who I am. I cannot become anyone else. Why should I be afraid to discover who I am?'

At that point Oedipus finally gets what he wants: the whole truth about himself, his origin and his history. He accepts it as the truth beyond doubt and beyond repair because he shares the moral judgment of his time (the mythological time). However, Oedipus has not received an answer to the question of his identity. He says, I am who I am. But who is he? Neither patricide nor incest is his character, his essence. He cannot stop questioning. Finally, in *Oedipus in Colonus*, he will answer this question before he dies, not in terms of the mythological story but in the spirit of an Athenian citizen. He was not the person guilty of patricide and incest, he is guilty of wanting to know. Consequently, tragedy and not myth, not even Solon's legends is the first source or resource of Athenian moral philosophy.

To add something to the theme of the birth of moral philosophy in tragedies, I will turn back briefly to Aeschylus' *Oresteia* and the surviving second part of another tragic trilogy, *Prometheus Unbound*. In Aeschylus' *Agamemnon* the first moral idea, presented by the chorus, after having recounted the sacrifice of Iphigenia by her father for the sake of his army, sounds, I believe, like something else. An ugly and evil deed begets an ugly and evil deed, the same is replicated, just as the good in the right home will beget good and beautiful descendants. The evil deed of Agamemnon (the sacrifice of his daughter) begot an evil deed and this again another evil deed. With Sophocles' *Antigone* the chain of evil deeds ends in Thebes. Yet, as far as Argos (contrary to Thebes) is concerned, Athena will stop the chain of evil deeds.

Orestes kills his mother Clytemnestra, knowing well what he was doing. His crime is even worse than that of Clytemnestra, since in killing her husband Agamemnon she is not killing a blood relative. How and on what moral ground could Athena throw her stone in favour of Orestes' acquittal, when the votes of yes and no were even? What were her moral reasons? Why did she side with a man against women? Before his matricide (in the second part of the trilogy, *The Libation Bearers*) Orestes says, 'Ares challenges Ares, Dike challenges <u>Dike</u>' (that is: there is justice on both sides). In response Electra (who is not as revengeful as in Sophocles' *Electra*) cries out: 'You gods, judge according to the right.' The question will be: what is right? Or rather: who decides upon right or wrong?

In the third part of the trilogy the Furies accuse Orestes before the new court directed by Athena. The Furies raise their accusation against Orestes. Athena says both parties need to argue their position. The verbal duel does not decide matters of right or wrong, only impartial judges can do this. Let us also listen to Orestes. That Orestes killed his mother and her lover is beyond doubt, yet Athena wants to know his motivation. Up to this point this seemed to be obvious: unjust revenge or misplaced vendetta. Sufficient in the tradition, not, however, before the court. What is Orestes' defence? He was blackmailed by Apollo, who threatened him with insufferable pain if he does not do it. An old defence always returning: I did what I did, but I did it under pressure and under command. The question remains as to whether the defence of Orestes is strong enough to curtail his punishment. Athena answers that she will select the best men of the state as a jury to decide. Apollo testifies as a witness. Yes, he was the one who put pressure on Orestes. Orestes asks why have the Furies not tortured his murderess mother? The answer: because it was not her blood relation whom she killed.

With this point the old and the new law collide. According to the new order murder is murder, whether the murdered is your blood relative or not. Orestes asks: had I the right to kill or not? Apollo argues that a mother is not really a mother. The real ancestor is the begetter, the father, who gives his seed. (It is at this point that interpreters talk about the conflict between matriarchy and patriarchy.) Yet as far as Athenian ethics and legal practices are concerned, the closing part of the *Oresteia* offers us a precise insight into Aristotle's ethics roughly a hundred years later. When is an actor entirely responsible for his deed? When his character, he himself is the source of his deed, by decision or by passion. Yet he is not fully responsible if he acted under heavy pressure. To return to the *Oresteia*: the command of a god, the threat of extreme pain count as heavy pressure. It is a mitigating circumstance.

This was written, performed and praised before the appearance of moral philosophy. Sophocles was a good citizen. Euripides and Socrates were contemporaries. The last of the great tragic poets and the first of the great philosophers were bad citizens and, allegedly, also friends. Socrates was murdered by the citizens of his state while Euripides migrated to Macedonia. Athens changed substantially after the Peloponnesian War. Although democracy was finally restored, it was corrupt and philistine. Socrates and Euripides were accused of the corruption of politics and the dissolution of morality, detected and unmasked. The comedy writer of the day, Aristophanes, ridiculed both of them in *The Clouds* and *The Frogs*.

Representative German thinkers since Winckelmann, especially the stars of classical German literature like Goethe and Schiller, imagined an ancient Greece of beauty and harmony. Their points of reference were the statues of the gods, of Apollo and of Aphrodite. How harmonious, how beautiful they were! Even their dramas based on Greek mythological themes like *Iphigenia in Tauris* by Goethe are classical in the sense of a statue. Nietzsche challenged this vision of the Greek way of life. There were two different life experiences of the ancient Greeks: one expressed in architecture and sculpture, the other in tragic poetry, a happy and an unhappy one, an optimistic and a pessimistic one, the Apollonian and the Dionysian. Nietzsche omits the point Aristotle made about the relation between work and audience, he concentrates rather on the presentation of the 'terrible,' on the ruse of unreason and on the chorus formulating it. He refers for example to a strophe from the chorus in Sophocles' *Oedipus in Colonus*, telling us that it is a blessing to die young, but the best is never to be born. (The context of this choral song is Oedipus's misdeed and his suffering as a grown and old man. For him, it would have been better to die young or not to be born. Not a single song of the chorus can be understood without its context.)

I already quoted at the beginning Hegel's words about philosophy always arriving late, painting grey in grey, and that tragedy blossoms before the appearance of the final philosophy. Nietzsche's story is more radical. It is not just that philosophy appeared and flourished at a time when tragedy was already in decline. In his mind it was philosophy that killed tragedy. Rationalism, rational thinking, kills tragedy. Socrates and his friend Euripides killed tragedy. One might even interpret Hegel's very rationalist dictum in Nietzsche's terms.

Philosophy (rationalism) paints grey in grey and this is why it kills tragedy that shines in several colours. Nietzsche speaks only of Greek tragedy in this context whereas Hegel includes Shakespeare in his general discussion on tragedy in his *Aesthetics*.

In *The Birth of Tragedy* Nietzsche dwells at some length on the Socrates/Euripides relationship. He disliked Euripides for putting the audience on the stage, that is, for reducing the great heroes or heroines, the gods and semigods of Greek mythology to one of them, no higher in stature and thinking than mortals. Maybe when Aristotle called Euripides the most tragic writer, this was not meant as a compliment. Greek tragedy died by suicide, according to Nietzsche, at the hand of Euripides. Euripides abandoned Dionysus, and he too was abandoned by Apollo. Nietzsche's description of the fate of tragedy is, in my mind, beautiful, passionate and also correct. In Euripides' poetry, says Nietzsche, Greeks lost their belief in their immortality, in their ideal past, and their ideal future. Is the speaker the cause of what they express? In Euripides, adds Nietzsche, 'feminine' fear arises from the terrible. He brings the terrible on the stage as just another critical thinker, like the rationalist Socrates.

If one interpreted Nietzsche in this sense as if the tragic heroes and heroines of Euripides are acting more rationally than the characters of Sophocles, one would be disappointed. Rather, the opposite is the case. The characters of Euripides are far more irrational than those of the classic tragic poets. Medea kills her own children, while Pentheus drugs himself and runs berserk to be murdered by his own mother. Nietzsche interprets *The Bacchae* as the poet Euripides bowing before the power of Dionysus. Yet, he always acknowledged his power. This was Euripides' true critical position, and this was his rationalism: to understand that understanding is impotent and the easy victim of the dark forces of Dionysus. Yes, Euripides hates Dionysus' power because this power of trance, obsession and intoxication robs men of even their common sense. The intoxicated become slaves of their hallucinations and their fanaticism. They cannot ask like Oedipus any questions about their real identity because they do not want to know the truth about themselves or about anything else.

Pentheus in *The Bacchae* becomes an easy prey of irrational forces, because he wants to spy on these forces by dressing as a woman. His fate reminds me of Thomas Mann's story *Mario and the Magician*. Here Dionysus is the magician and Pentheus plays the role of the Roman gentleman who finally begins to dance just as the magician commands. Who says only 'no' never 'yes' will always lose against devilish powers. Maybe this is indeed rationalism: the insight into the powerlessness of reason. Maybe this is what Socrates also realized while standing before his judges. Rationality is the loser. What else made Euripides the last tragic poet and Socrates the first philosopher the twin stars in ailing Athens in opposition to their world? A sceptic or ironical attitude towards the holy tradition. Socrates was accused of neglecting or even defying the gods of the city by obeying a personal god, his *daimon* and his character.

A philosopher always has the privilege of creating his own world. The tragic author in Athens did not share this privilege since he had to borrow his plot from mythology. Euripides had to as well. Yet, when it came to the question 'who is who,' he added, 'as they say' or 'so it is believed' as a kind of pre-Cartesian sceptic. Unlike his great predecessors, Euripides was a pessimist. He lived in a collapsing world and he felt its collapse. If some of his tragedies end on a positive tone, this occurs through outside intervention, a *deus ex machina*, for it does not follow from the logic of the plot.

As far as the so-called 'feminine' side of Euripides is concerned, Nietzsche could have referred to one of his own thoughts: that suffering is not terrible, yet senseless suffering is. Neither the suffering of Oedipus and Orestes, nor that of Antigone and Prometheus was senseless in the tragedies of the first two tragic poets. But there is senseless suffering many times in Euripides' tragedies. For example, in a very 'feminine' play, *The Women of Troy,* the women of Troy are taken as slaves by the Greek conquerors who distribute them among the army. The chorus of captive women laments together with Hecuba, their former queen. Hecuba lost her husband and all her sons. Only two of her daughters remain: Cassandra will be taken as Agamemnon's concubine, her other daughter Polyxena has been killed at Achilles' tomb. This is the first totally senseless murder in a tragedy. Another senseless murder will follow. The Greeks kill Andromache's little son just because he is Hector's son. He is thrown from a cliff into the abyss. This is no longer Greek mythology, this is Shakespeare (for example, the murder of the little princes in *Richard III*). Listening to the laments of the Trojan women, one easily associates the lament of the three women, mother, former queen and wife in *Richard III*. Hecuba buries her grandson in the robes of a dead soldier. Troy is in flames. 'Gods, Gods, where are you? Why should I clamour to the gods? We called on them before and no one heard our call ... There your way lies – forward into slavery!' This suffering is indeed senseless. We do not know about Socrates' understanding of tragedy. We only know what Plato put into his mouth.

The young Plato wanted to be a tragic poet, yet after having met Socrates he gave up this goal and started to write philosophical dialogues instead. By doing so he created new characters using the Greek language to create a new literary genre. At the end of *The Symposium*, Socrates enters into a discussion about poetry. He suggests that comedy and tragedy could be written by the same poet. This was unheard of in Athens and in the whole ancient world. We know that two thousand years after Plato, Shakespeare was the poet who did it. However, the outlandish suggestions of Plato's Socrates did not have in mind a kind of ancient Shakespeare, but a new genre, his invention, philosophy. Philosophy is, indeed, a literary genre that at the very beginning fulfils the role of both tragedy and comedy. For example, in Socrates' apology he chooses death willingly, seemingly a tragic conclusion, yet he supports his decision in words full of sarcasm and irony well suited to a comedy. This combination will disappear with Aristotle to reappear in one or other works of future philosophers.

The gist of the matter is that even without being tragic or comic philosophers took the torch called immortality from writers of tragedy. After Euripides tragedy writers just repeated the tradition, whereas philosophers innovated by conceptualizing a world already in decay. Plato knew it. Even though he was still the son of the polis of Pericles, he was aware of the truth that Pericles' world is forever gone. Aristotle, a stranger in Athens and everywhere, no longer suffered from this loss. He was at home in Athens and everywhere where they spoke Greek or later Latin and discussed philosophy. He really painted – as Hegel remarked – grey in grey, since the darkness was already setting on both democracy and tragedy.

Let me return to the birth of philosophy, to Plato's Socrates. We know that Plato was no friend of poetry, neither of Homer nor of tragic authors. Poets lie. They lie about the gods, ascribing immoral thoughts and deeds to them, and they lie also in presenting something that does not exist, copying a copy of ideas, the opinions and the acts of the cave dwellers. By dismissing the myths (as Socrates expresses himself in *Phaedrus*) Plato creates his own personal myths, also sometimes ironical ones.

Plato was the first who spoke of art as mimesis, imitation, a conception further developed by Aristotle. However, there was one unique aspect in Plato's interpretation of mimesis: he applied his theory to acting and to actors. In Plato's view one should remain oneself and should never present a person other than oneself. Acting is not only cheating, pretending, it also destroys a person's personality. This interpretation of acting and the role of the actor will later play a role in theories of dramatic art. In the Middle Ages the judgment of Plato was generally accepted. Acting was regarded as frivolous and undignified. This perception changes very slowly even after the re-emergence and increasing popularity of theatre in the Renaissance. Not even in Shakespeare's time, the time of the blossoming of theatre, was an actor regarded as a gentleman. Theatre acting was also later, many times, prohibited as an immoral, seductive and dangerous profession.

3 Shakespeare: Tragedy and History

The second greatest period of tragedy was the offspring of the second greatest leap in human histories: the leap from traditional societies into modern societies. There were several radical changes, even revolutions earlier. The acceptance of Christianity in Rome was the most important among them. Yet, despite these revolutions, the essential structure, the stratification model of societies, remained the same. All of them were traditional world orders. Slavery was subsequently replaced by serfdom, clientele by bondsmen. The traditions were different, but not the fundamental social structures. Briefly, this meant that the place where a person was born almost entirely determined the place that person would occupy in the social division of labour throughout his or her whole life. Not just how and whether needs should be satisfied was allocated according to different social strata and gender, but the needs themselves. To use a term coined by Marx: these societies were *naturwüchsig*, that is, naturally grown, reproduced by family ties, earth and place. To love parents was natural, the fate of people was unchangeable, tradition sacred and decreed by gods or by God.

No surprise that Plato and Aristotle remained 'the' philosophers for more than a thousand years. Even scientific knowledge was based on Aristotle and on other ancient sages. There were changes, yet the main structure of the European world remained unchanged. And then suddenly an entirely new world emerged. A world where the word 'new' was no longer suspect, the old no longer respected, where the traditional order – all traditional orders – were shaken, where people no longer knew who they were, where they did not understand the world anymore. Where traditional loyalties were questioned, where family ties could be replaced by other ties, like friendship or personal love, or broken for the sake of personal ambition or passion. This was the world of Elizabethan tragedy.

The political form of the state where modern tragedy emerged was absolute monarchy. Absolute monarchy was the political bridge between hereditary monarchy and the republic. Constitutional monarchy, as it emerged in Britain, was already regarded as a kind of republic. Absolute monarchy was born in war (religious wars included) in England and later in France and ended in revolutions. Between war and revolution, in times of stability, drama, tragedy and comedy alike, flourished: in England under Elisabeth and the early years of Stuart rule and in France, under Louis XIV and Louis XV.

In his tragedies Marlowe put on the stage the three greatest powers of his age: the power of money, the power of knowledge, and political power – the latter on the model of Tamerlane, a self-made tyrant, and an 'unnatural' ruler. The Shakespearian tragedies and comedies grew out of the fertile soil of the second dramatic change in human histories. I emphasize both tragedies and comedies, since Shakespeare (and others among his contemporaries) fulfilled Plato's wish: he was the author of both tragedies and comedies. More, he did something unimaginable for ancient tragedians. A few of his tragedies also included comic scenes, like the scene of the night watchman in *Macbeth*. This innovation was a poetic reflection on the heterogeneity of Shakespeare's world: that some of Shakespeare's comedies ended almost tragically was in itself no novelty, following the model of Roman comic poets. See for example *Twelfth Night* or *As You Like It*, a play modelled on Terence.

Before beginning to speak of the modern conflict between the two colliding worlds in Shakespeare, let me return briefly to the three conditions and the five constituents common to all tragedies: The three necessary conditions are: theatre, work, audience. All three conditions were met in Shakespeare's time to an extent unknown since the demise of Rome. Theatre slowly became a London institution, replacing the market as the space for shows. Theatres were no longer amphitheatres, but solid buildings created or reused for this very function. As we know, the actors did not play in masks, and as a result facial expression became as important for actors as the modulation of voice. The audience was even more mixed than it used to be in Athens or in Hellenistic cities. It included all 'social strata' from the Queen to labourers, and – contrary to Athens – also both genders and all age groups. Theatre again became the institution of the public sphere.

And what about the five constituents of tragedies? The 'general state of the world' was calling for tragedy for the second time. Entirely heterogeneous worlds collided on the stage, worlds presenting and representing entirely different, mostly incompatible ideas, thoughts, morals, convictions and styles of life. Passions and convictions were represented by actions and speech acts of individual characters, all of whom put everything at stake, mobilized by their subjective pathos. *Agon* (verbal duels mostly between two people), the collision between the individual carriers of different visions, was back again. The conflict between two essentially different values or ideas, between the old and the new was again fought out before an audience on the stage. The motif of *deinos*, that is, the vision of the human condition, is again the fundamental problem raised and answered with a question mark: is the human race magnificent, terrible, or both?

Philosophical ruminations and reflections occupy a central place in all Shakespearian tragedies. The chorus does not present the questions, puzzles and the meaning of human existence, does not summarize them as in the Greek plays (even if there is a pseudo-chorus like that of the witches in *Macbeth*), now the main characters or other important characters present them in their monologues. Monologue replaces the chorus as the philosophical voice, to formulate, praise or bemoan the tragic conflict taking place on the stage. The main actors of the play, while listening to their internal voice in solitude before making a decisive choice or after confronting a fatal one, are ruminating between yes and no, reflecting on life, nature and the destiny of the human condition before our eyes. The monologue situation itself stands for the overall importance of individuality in modern life. There is no fate or destiny that overshadows the life of the hero from his birth, even if coincidences and accidents can play a similar role (*Romeo and Juliet*, *King Lear*). Still, characters are the final sources of their destiny and the destiny of those close to them.

But what about Hegel's suggestion of reconciliation in the closing part of all tragedies, ancient and modern? Not all Greek tragedies end with reconciliation, not even those of Sophocles (see *Antigone*). In Shakespeare, however, it looks as if a kind of reconciliation does close all his plays. Tragedy, at least modern tragedy, ends with death, mostly not with just one single death but with many. However, after the death of several characters, good and evil alike, after the collapse of an evil world, a new more promising world appears on the stage. According to Jan Kott in *Shakespeare Our Contemporary* this is only seemingly so. Reconciliation is formal, since we do not know (except in the case of the second part of *Henry IV* and *Richard III*) whether the new, victorious king will not be as evil as the former, or at least not as weak in facing the powers of evil. Will the same story begin once again? The audience, always seeking for hope and satisfaction, answers the question. They are normally satisfied that the worst is over.

Like all tragic poets, Shakespeare borrowed his plots from the past. From myths, legends, histories. Poetry changes them all. Shakespeare wrote in verse, so whenever a scene was written in prose it meant something. The craftsmen mainly speak in prose and in comedies almost everyone does. Shakespeare's tragedies do not resemble ancient ones in many important ways, although the three conditions and the five constituents of all tragedies are the same as they used to be in Athens. Shakespeare's audience did not care for this difference. They were mostly not familiar with ancient tragedies. The art experts, the theoreticians and the cultured public could not, however, easily reconcile themselves with these 'barbarian' works. Shakespeare's works were censored, abbreviated, cut, some expressions and scenes were entirely omitted or 'gentrified' (also in many 19th century translations), and the ends changed. In general, literary texts (dramas, novels) were not regarded as holy and untouchable as they became from the 20th century onwards.

It seems as if philosophy had to reach the century of Enlightenment to start understanding Shakespeare's genius. The recognition was also delayed by

French classic theatre, since Corneille and Racine remained true to the conventions of ancient tragic poetry – although they were modern authors. It was Lessing who called Shakespeare the real and the only authentic follower of ancient Greek tragic poetry, placing him much above French classicism.

It was fashion, and I think that it still is, to cast doubt on Shakespeare's authorship. How could a person who knew little Latin and less Greek, who was not a cultivated nobleman, and about whom we know so little, write those plays? There were times when even educated people believed that Lord Bacon had written them under the name of 'Shakespeare.' This is of course nonsense. Yet, that Francis Bacon had something in common with Shakespeare's view of the world is beyond doubt. He was the first philosopher who greeted the modern world in his philosophy. He contrasted the new with the old, siding with the new. The titles of his most important works also suggest this: *Novum organum*, *The New Atlantis* and *Instauratio Magna*. Yet the way Shakespeare and Bacon saw the world shows very little resemblance. For Bacon the new was entirely unproblematic and better in everything than the old, whereas for Shakespeare, the tragic poet, neither the old nor the new was unproblematic. Even if he sides in most conflicts with the new, this is rarely unconditional endorsement or as free of moral contradiction as in *Romeo and Juliet* or in several comedies. The philosophers who stood closest to Shakespeare's vision were the Renaissance ones. Machiavelli whom he knew only from hearsay, and Montaigne whom he knew and liked. Many kings in Shakespeare's historical plays are very 'Machiavellian' even if not in the spirit of the real Machiavelli. The portrayal of the friendship between Hamlet and Horatio was inspired by Montaigne's essay on friendship. One can understand why Shakespeare was 'discovered' in the Enlightenment.

History, the 'times out of joint,' stood for Shakespeare in the centre of his poetic interest, not only in his tragedies but also sometimes in his non-tragic dramas, the so called romances. Early modern art theorists had great problems with Shakespeare as far as genre definition was concerned. What about the unity of action, place and time and the sacred rules of dramatic poems in Aristotle? One can, perhaps, read the trilogies of Greek classics (for example, *Oedipus the King*, *Oedipus in Colonus*, *Antigone* and the *Oresteia*) as one single tragedy in three acts. Read in this way, the unity of time and place does not apply to Greek tragedies either. Where then is the difference between Sophocles and Shakespeare? Or, consider just another Aristotelian idea, according to which a tragic hero cannot be entirely evil or entirely virtuous, rather he has to commit a tragic mistake. What then about the virtuous naivety of Shakespeare's Henry VI or Juliet? Do they commit tragic mistakes? Or the radically evil character of Richard III or Lady Macbeth? What remains of divine interventions? It is vain to hunt for similarities, where the ultimate difference is beyond doubt.

In Shakespeare God is a spectator and not an actor, whereas in ancient tragedies gods were actors and interfered in the action repeatedly. For example, Apollo commanded Orestes to kill his mother and he acted also as witness at Orestes' trial. Ancient gods set limits to actions. Yet Shakespeare's God never interferes directly in the tragic development of a plot. He simply lets men and women choose according to the virtues and vices of their character. The divine laws and commandments are known by all the characters. When a King is unjustly dethroned or killed, he can refer to the King of kings, but this King of kings lets his creatures play their roles: to obey or to disobey divine moral laws. This is a matter of their conscience. Everyone is free to choose. There is not even a *deus absconditus* (hidden God) or an actor as the mouthpiece of God. There is no prophet and no sage. Is there then no limit? The times, the situations, and their embodiments in conflicting actors set the limit. This is a historical world, not a mythological one. Not because the stories are taken from chronicles, but because the regard of the author is historical. The world changes for the better or for the worse by human action or by the inability to act. The outcome is never entirely foreseeable, yet after a while it becomes at least partially so, for the logic of characters leads to one outcome or the other and to a new historical situation, while embodying the spirit of the state of the world. (Even great Shakespeare lovers do not understand why he 'kills' Cordelia. This is Euripides, not Shakespeare!)

Shakespeare came earlier than Rousseau, Condorcet, Lessing or Kant, and yet he already knew everything to be known about history. Shakespeare came earlier than the philosophers also in another respect. He came after Luther (Hamlet arrives from Wittenberg) and he was interested in the 'internal spaces' of men. The function of monologues is not just to occupy the place of wisdom and poetry of the chorus but also to express and manifest the internal spaces of men. There is no psychology in Greek drama, yet in Shakespeare (and Marlowe) it stands at the centre of the plot. The internal space can be almost self-identical in both evil and in good characters, yet normally it is split and changing and sometimes radically (*King Lear* or *Richard II*).

Philosophical anthropology developed only in the 17th and 18th centuries. It was unknown to the ancients (the slave and the master could not belong to the same cluster), whereas in mediaeval philosophy our original sin was presupposed, even if not necessarily also as hereditary sin. Modern philosophy vacillated between Hobbes and Rousseau. In Hobbes' anthropology humanity was originally brutal, murderous or evil, becoming law abiding and peaceful after the social contract. In Rousseau humankind was originally blessed with universal empathy and only society transformed it from good to evil, due to egoism, comparison, love of luxury. Needless to say, neither Hobbes nor Rousseau meant to write history: they presented models of human nature. Philosophers, due to the requirement of their genre, speak about human nature in general, in Shakespeare, however, there is no human in general to be born either good or evil, since every human being is different, each in their own way good or evil or neither in a concrete world and in a concrete situation. One can have the impression that Shakespeare simply threw a few very different characters into a situation in order to find out how they would act. He waited for the result curiously just as his God did.

In ancient theatre masks served the purpose of showing which known character the actor plays, or at least what his function as a character is (as in Aristophanes). Precisely this is excluded by Shakespeare. The unique character has to be expressed by his or her body, and primarily by the face, not only for the obvious purpose that we, the spectators, should guess at the beginning what kind of person is on the stage, what kind of role he or she is going to play, but also for another purpose: that other characters also see the faces and read or misread a character from the face. Not only the spectator needs to recognize the hypocrite, but also his or her alleged friend on the stage. The characters in the play have to learn whom they can confide in and whom not, who is a flatterer and who is sincere. They have to learn how to hide their own feelings if necessary, as does Hamlet.

Know thyself! was the guideline for Greek philosophers and tragic poets as well: so it remains in Shakespeare! Who am I? What am I? A few Shakespearian characters, like Hamlet or Lear, constantly ask themselves these questions and give different answers. The Delphi inscription said: know thyself and honour Apollo. The second part of the injunction for the moderns is different, however: know thyself and know the other. There are characters in Shakespeare who are great readers of human character, like Julius Caesar or Hamlet, and there are those who are bad at it, like Lear or Othello. This is why the knowledge of character plays such an important role in Shakespeare, not just in tragedies, but also in comedies and in romances. Trust and distrust are equally important, and one should know whom to trust and whom to distrust. To refer back (or forward) to Hegel: character is not identical with individuality. No question, that Orestes or Antigone are characters, yet since they carried a universal message, they could not be individuals. They are lacking the internal spaces. This is why they are plastic, like statues, whereas Shakespeare's heroes are rather depicted graphically as individuals.

We do not know who we are and what are we capable or not capable of doing. The whole identity crisis behind all Shakespearian dramas centres around the question: what is natural? Is there a law of nature standing above all other laws? Is the traditional natural? The commitment to natural law against tradition is formulated many times by one or other characters in Shakespeare. The best known is Juliet on the balcony. What is Capulet? Montague? Just names! Love is the law of nature, of the body, of the soul and not a name! Or: is the love of a patrician Venetian girl for a black general unnatural, as her father believes? Edmund in *King Lear* refers to the same law of nature as Juliet: is a bastard inferior to a legal offspring? And Shylock? Has a Jew not the same natural constitution as a Christian? It is very important that while Shakespeare formulates the fundamental conflict, he does not attribute moral superiority to either side. Juliet is good, Edmund is evil, but both refer to nature against convention. Romeo and Juliet choose love against all odds, but so also do Suffolk and Margaret, an otherwise unpleasant pair (in *King Henry VI*). I say only in brackets that the differentiation appeared already in the Sophist school but had at that time no effect on tragic poetry. Identity crises and the conflict between two interpretations of the 'natural' are connected in modern tragedy. Passions lead sometimes to evil deeds and sometimes to good ones. The 'nothing too much' imperative does not fit into Shakespeare's world: passions are welcome, and sometimes the question of right or wrong cannot be decided.

There are two hierarchies in Shakespeare, one moral, the other of grandeur. These two are rarely identical. Hamlet is at the top of the grandeur hierarchy, whereas Horatio is at the top of the moral hierarchy, even Hamlet says so. Julius Caesar is at the top of the grandeur hierarchy, and Brutus is on the top of the moral hierarchy. I mentioned the Hegelian reconciliation at the end of Shakespeare's dramas. It is generally an interesting reconciliation. Either the new wins at the end or the old and the new find a common ground. But whichever way, something is always lost: grandeur. Not morality but grandeur. With the exception of *Richard III*: here morality and history win the peace together, if not also grandeur.

Shakespeare was a unique genius, no one can be compared to him. He created worlds in a way no one else has. Kant distinguished in his *Critique of Judgment* between taste and genius. The genius does not follow the rules of the genre but creates new ones. The learned strata are learned because they have taste. They rarely recognize genius. The London audience of all social strata liked Shakespeare. Even the cultural elite loved him and visited his theatre, although they had no high opinion of him. Just as the cultural elite of the 20th century read Agatha Christie but did not consider her novels literature. Shakespeare's genius was only discovered at the time of Enlightenment. Yet even then, tragedies like *Richard III* bothered the interpreters. How can an evil man, a villain, be a tragic hero? The answer is, in my view, that he is not the tragic hero. This tragedy is the last of the tragedies of the War of the Roses (although written earlier than the others). The tragic heroes of these plays are the two royal families, who destroy each other and themselves just like the royal families of Thebes or Argos. Only that the 'state of the world' is now entirely different. The Aristotelian rules could not be followed in the new state of the world. However, when we move from London to Paris and Versailles half a century later it seems as if they could.

4   French Classicism: Tragedy and Passion

French dramatists took Aristotle's theory of tragedy and of drama in general as a valid and eternal yardstick. The idea of the eternal stood with them higher than temporality. Contrary to Shakespeare, they were not motivated to understand and to depict history. Like the Greeks, they wanted to put human nature and destiny on stage, as presented and represented in the story by single human beings. Still, they also reflected upon their own times, sometimes on purpose, sometimes not, and they could not help seeing the single men and women with the eyes of their own times, not just as characters but also as individuals.

Although it is in vogue to speak about Corneille and Racine as if they were twins, despite the fact that they were competing with one another, they were very different, not just poetically but also philosophically. Shakespeare was not directly related to Francis Bacon, but Corneille and Racine were directly related to the French philosophy of their times: to Descartes and to Pascal. If I were malicious, I would now apply Nietzsche's remark on Euripides to the French classics. Just as Socrates appeared on the stage of Euripides, as Nietzsche suggests, Descartes, or at least the spirit of Descartes appeared on the stage of Corneille, together with Pascal on the stage of Racine.

If one reads Corneille, especially *Le Cid*, *Cinna* or *Horatius*, stories borrowed from Spanish and Roman lore, one reads three masterpieces of rational argumentation. Take for example in *Le Cid* the scene of the lovers, Don Rodrigo and Ximena, after Rodrigo kills her father who insulted Rodrigo's father. Both offer a chain of rational arguments to prove why they did what they did and what they are going to do. *Agon* is a decisive constituent of every drama, but in the Greek *agon*, even if the person represents a traditional virtue or expresses an injury (*Antigone* or *Prometheus Unbound*) the argument is not entirely rational and never as long. In Corneille, the arguments are completely rational like the arguments of Descartes in for example his *Meditations on a First Philosophy*. Standing before a choice, the actors argue for one and then for another option. If there is such a thing as a completely rational choice, you will find it in Corneille. The heroes talk about their emotions such as love, yet this emotion is just one piece in the argument and never decisive. Even monologues are characterised by rational argumentation. The so-called double bind is also formulated in a chain of arguments, for example by Sabina in *Horatius* when she has to choose between husband and brother. The audience ceases to be confronted by embodied souls, just by their words, although with constant reference to a very personal, very individual experience, again like Descartes in his *Discourse on Method*.

The relations between philosophers and tragic works are also mutual. Montesquieu had Corneille in mind when he distinguished between the main moral motivation in a republic and in a monarchy. In a republic, he says, the main moral motivation is virtue, whereas in monarchy it is honour. In Corneille it is always honour. All his heroes and heroines defend their honour. The way representative others look at you, see and judge you, this is what you are. A shame culture, not yet combined with conscience culture, as was the case in Shakespeare and will be the case in Racine.

In Corneille's *Cinna*, where the topic is close to that of a Shakespearian drama, Emilia, the lover of Cinna, who conspires against Augustus to restore the republic, ruminates: 'your life maybe in danger, yet not your honour.' Neither *Le Cid* nor *Cinna* is in my view a tragedy, rather they are romantic plays, even melodramas (*Le Cid* was later a popular opera by Massenet). In *Le Cid* Rodrigo becomes a national hero and finally gets his beloved as well, whereas in *Cinna* Emilia changes her mind and recognizes the blessing of Augustus' monarchy. In *Horatius* at the end, the old Horatius gives everyone his just deserts. None of these dramas fits the tradition of tragedy. The Christian drama *Polyeucte* alone looks to me to be an exception. I mentioned earlier that Biblical stories are great topics for oratorios or passion plays, but not for tragedies. As opposed to *Le Cid*, *Cinna*, and *Horatius*, *Polyeucte* ends with undeserved deaths: the death of two innocents. Yet these two innocents are confident that by dying as martyrs they will gain entrance to Heaven and eternal happiness as reward for their martyrdom. There can be no *catharsis* in the soul of the spectators, for they do not fear going to Heaven and do not feel empathy for those who have guaranteed access to it. This is a drama, where not the dying victims but the victimizer becomes the tragic hero. The Roman Severus, under the influence of the Christian martyrs, changes his mind but not by becoming a Christian himself. What has happened? What follows from his change of mind? He declares tolerance! There should be no interference with each other's faith.

In Corneille's time this was more important than ever. Both the audience and the Catholic king were addressed: the fight between Catholic and Protestant led to the murder of the innocents, written in a time that would end in the French king repealing the edict of Nantes and expelling the Protestants.

Please change your mind! This was a political declaration, driven by fear of the revival of religious war and empathy with the victims.

Racine was an entirely different tragic poet. He took the interpretation of Aristotle's *Poetics* by Boileau seriously: the threefold unity of time, place and action such that the action of a tragedy should develop at the one place in one day.

Two among Racine's tragedies were new versions of Greek mythological stories. His favourite author was Euripides, and this already tells us a lot, given that Euripides changed the traditional plots, sometimes essentially. Racine praises Euripides for this, since this is also what he is doing. His mythological characters are Greek only in name. They are modern French men and women playing old stories. And so are Roman historical figures like Britannicus, or even the Biblical heroine Athalie.

Shakespeare reflected on tragedy, drama and acting through his characters (for example Hamlet), whereas Racine wrote prefaces to his dramas. There he reflects on his own interpretation: why have I developed my story the way I did? Who is the real protagonist of my stories? In the preface to *Berenice*, a Roman historical tragedy, he even questions the Aristotelian rules. He wants to emulate the ancients first and foremost through the simple plot of the drama. The most important rule of a drama, according to Racine, is to please and to move. In the preface to *Phaedra* Racine praises his own work: he has never written such a good tragedy as this one! Why? Because in this play the thought of evil is as evil as the evil deed itself. This idea was entirely alien to the Greek way of thinking and also to Shakespeare. Theorists refer in this connection to the influence of Port Royal and Jansenism, the pietistic version of Catholicism in conflict with the Jesuits of the court, since Racine was close to the Jansenists. His conviction was that tragedy had to educate the audience in keeping with the aims of Port Royal, even though they, generally, condemned theatre.

Yet what about the passions? For the Greeks the virtuous person finds the middle measure between too much and too little, the way Aristotle saw it in his *Nichomachean Ethics*. Yet, Racine lives in Descartes' time. We know that Jansenists, like Pascal, disapproved of Descartes' philosophy, but in his *Passions of the Soul* Descartes made one of the experiences of his time explicit: there are no evil passions except fanaticism. The moral problem is not with passions but with the object of a passion. One cannot love God too much or friends, there is no excess here. A passion is wrong if it is oriented to the wrong target (as in Racine Phaedra's love for Hippolytus). And even if we move from Descartes to Pascal, we encounter a similar problem. Pascal distinguished between the logic of the mind and the logic of the heart. The latter is, according to him, substantially good, not just because it is related to the right target.

Just as Shakespeare knew more about history than any philosopher in his time, so Racine knew more about passions than the philosophers of his time, even more than Descartes. He knew about the problematic character of feelings. Surely in his comedies Shakespeare knew it too, enough to refer to Titania 'enamoured with an ass' in *Midsummer Night's Dream*, not in his tragedies, however. There lovers are good or evil (the latter, for example, in *Macbeth*), love can be cheated, disappointed, forbidden but the feeling of love, even the passion of love remains in itself unproblematic in the soul of the lovers. In the case of Shakespeare modern tragedy opens the internal rooms of the character. In their monologues the actors, especially the protagonists, make confessions to the audience and tell us about their intentions, their inner feelings and doubts. No one in the drama has access to their secrets, to their internal space, only we, the voyeurs and perhaps God, also a voyeur, do. In Corneille we get access to the inner thoughts of the characters through the chain of arguments and through the long ruminations of the actors ending in a rational choice.

In Racine, however, we already step into the pages of 18th and 19th century novels or short stories, into the world of problematic and also uncontrollable emotions, which destroy the person, make a joke of the *ego cogito*, of self-knowledge and self-understanding. The question: what I am? cannot be answered and the actor is aware that it cannot be answered. Rarely before Racine could anyone ask the question about the identity of the hero or heroine in a tragedy, since this was self-evident. In Racine, however, it is not self-evident at all. Who is the tragic figure then? Whose tragedy are we witnessing? In a tragedy this needs to be answered. *Athalie* is not a tragedy because the Biblical story ends with Joas, the heir to David, ascending the throne just as the real God wins against false gods. To repeat, redemptive history fits oratorio but not tragedy.

Racine's *Andromache*, like Euripedes' *Women of Troy*, is set after the defeat of Troy. One of the victors is Orestes, in love with Hermione, daughter of Helen, another is Pyrrhus, son of Achilles, the murderer of Hector. Pyrrhus loves Andromache, the widow of Hector. The enslaved Andromache defends her dead husband's memory and the life of their son. Something unheard of happens: Pyrrhus says that by seeing Andromache's plight he begins to feel pangs of conscience for having destroyed Troy. Listen: pangs of conscience, because of winning a ten-year war against enemies and destroying them? What an un-Greek feeling! Echoing Euripides, the recurring theme is the terror of war, yet this time from the mouth of a victor. Andromache asks her rival Hermione, who loves Pyrrhus and is betrothed to him, to help save her son. Andromache's only desire is to save Hector's son and to remain loyal to Hector as well. After several threats finally Pyrrhus proposes to make Andromache queen if she agrees to marry him, otherwise her son will be killed. She seemingly agrees and decides to commit suicide after the wedding. However, her purpose is crossed by another love-hatred story. Hermione loves Pyrrhus and hates him at the same time as she hates Andromache. Orestes loves Hermione and will do everything for her. She asks him to kill Pyrrhus. Pyrrhus is murdered but Orestes comes too late. Hermione commits suicide and Andromache will become queen. Racine's drama ends here. Who is the tragic heroine of this tragedy?

The ancients would say of course Andromache! She is like Antigone. She has one virtue: unconditional loyalty to the memory of her husband and his son. What would the moderns say? Hermione of course! Andromache survives and she even becomes queen without losing her virtue. Hermione loses everything, love, throne and her life. Moreover, she is responsible for her own fate. Not by committing a tragic mistake, not by following an outdated tradition, not by listening to bad advice, not by being betrayed, not even in a fit of rage, but just because she is carried away by contradictory uncontrollable passions. Because she loses control of her conflicting inner emotions, as we see also later in Racine's greatest tragedy, *Phaedra*.

In *Berenice* there is no question about the identity of the tragic heroine (if this drama is considered to be a tragedy at all). The Jewish queen Berenice renounces the prospect of marriage to Titus, the emperor, not because she feels it wrong but because she has no option. Titus chooses reasons of state over love. The collision between love and honour would have fitted better Corneille's pen but poetry above all. Berenice's words of farewell are Racine through and through, matched only once much later in Goethe's *Iphigenia in Tauris*.

In *Britannicus*, which Racine borrowed from Tacitus, Britannicus is not the central figure, he is rather the innocent and naive victim of Nero. Nero is perhaps the central figure, yet he is not the tragic hero, just a budding tyrant, a Richard III in the making. Contrary to Richard, however, he has not chosen himself as a villain and he is just evil in *statu nascendi*, who will become evil as he grows up. The tragic heroine in *Britannicus* is Nero's mother Agrippina, who commits the tragic mistake of doing everything in her power to put her son on the throne by cheating Britannicus of the imperial power that her husband, his father Claudius, wanted him to inherit. Agrippina is a kind of magician's apprentice, who lets the evil spirit out of the bottle and will be unable to control it. Of course, she does not know yet at this time that she herself will be murdered by her son, but Racine and his audience knew it. This is close to the Aristotelian model: she will be the victim of her tragic mistake. The other heroine of the tragedy, Junia, who loves the murdered Britannicus, is a non-tragic victim, who escapes from Nero to become a Vestal Virgin. The network of conspiracies in the imperial court, the corruption and flattery of advisers was not news for the spectators, but rather a mirror in which they recognize themselves or their enemies. The mutual, sometimes inherited, hatred of princes and nobles in Shakespeare becomes here the competition of petty, interest-driven conspirators at the imperial court. Even the advisers of the tyrant are presented as little conspirators, flatterers, devoid even of the grandeur of evil. This is the court of Louis XIV, as Racine under the influence of Port Royal saw it.

Racine explains in his Preface why he changed Euripides' tragedy by rescuing Phaedra from the crime of slandering Hippolytus to Theseus, her husband. In Euripides the accusation follows from her crazy, irrational passion, infringing the norm of 'nothing too much,' similar to Medea killing her sons. Nothing too much, the middle measure, no longer applies to passions in the time of Descartes' *Passions of the Soul* and Spinoza's *Ethics*. Racine did not know these works, but he perceived the spirit of the times. Hegel's dictum that without passions nothing great takes place in history was already felt and sometimes even formulated. Passions are not by definition irrational, even if they contradict common sense, as in the case of *Don Quixote*. They can be, however, self-destructive: love, hatred, jealousy are the most self-destructive emotions.

The passions played a minor role in Greek drama unless connected to political power. This is true even in Shakespeare's historical dramas and tragedies, unless directly connected to political power. *Romeo and Juliet* and *Othello* are exceptions. Jealousy, political and personal, sexual or nonsexual, is already a main motivation in Euripides' tragedies. Sexual love mainly as a matter of the body was rather the 'property' of comedies. In French classical drama the passion of love (amour passion) moved to the centre of tragic plots just as it also became central in the modern social imagination. This is no longer love of God, love of family, love of our country, of our lords, our spouse, our concubine, it is love not in the plural but in the singular. Free love, that is, a freely chosen love for a person of the other gender, is a sexual and exclusive passion. Amour passion moved to the centre of drama together with honour in Corneille to become the centre of tragedy altogether in Racine.

An all-important exclusive passion against convention, habit, custom, interest, ethics – or even law, this was the turning point. At the same time exclusive love as the condition of marriage, this new bourgeois idea, began to dominate the poetic and narrative imagination. Love and monogamy became related, at least in the value system. Yet, 'romantic love' challenged this too. From the representative novels of the 18th century like *The New Heloise* and *Werther*, up to the 'social novels' by Jane Austen, no work of literature, be it drama, novel and poetry, could have 'survived' without a love story. All this began with Racine, especially with *Phaedra*. Phaedra stands for love against the law, against marital ties and it is love for her stepson, the son of her husband Theseus. It is an 'oedipal passion' to speak with Freud. A passion that is known and felt as undignified by Phaedra, not just because of its irresistible character but also because her love is not only unrequited but despised by the object of her love, who loves someone else. Spinoza wrote that reason cannot conquer passion, only an opposite and stronger passion can. Phaedra, however, is possessed by one passion alone. No duty or fear for her honour can prevent this sole passion from ruling and ruining her. There is no contrary passion she fights for, no passion to conquer her dominating passion and desire. Therefore, the conflict is internal, as long as Phaedra is ruled by her desire alone. It is 'externalized' by Oinone, Phaedra's nurse. She accuses Hippolytus of the crime that Phaedra has committed to his father Theseus. Hippolytus dies, even if not by Phaedra's hand, as a result of her uncontrollable desire and Oinone's accusation.

The ending of this tragedy reminds us of Othello, another victim of a passion. Phaedra confesses and she even admits that she is responsible for Oinone's crime. And after her admission of guilt, like Othello she commits suicide. Racine pointed to the difference when he compared his version to that of Euripides, where Phaedra herself makes the false but fatal accusation. Othello murders Desdemona but Phaedra does not murder anyone. But one never knows the consequences of an evil wish. Who is responsible? Gods or fate, or just an accident or human nature or perhaps the credulity of Theseus or Onione's misplaced loyalty? Or Phaedra, the woman, who was cursed by women's fate in being left alone by an ungrateful husband in his house as a prisoner, a prey to unfulfilled desire and imagination? Guilty or not guilty? Who is guilty?

PART 2

Drama and Philosophy

1   Bourgeois Drama

I mentioned several times that according to Aristotle the hero or heroine of a tragedy should stand higher than the spectators. This was understood as meaning that only kings, queens, princes, princesses can be the central tragic characters. Philosophers of the Enlightenment challenged this view. In Paris in the 1750s, we witness the emergence of modern drama and simultaneously the end of tragedy. The genres of serious drama, drama and tragicomedy will dominate the stages of Europe up to the 20th century. They no longer stage the clashes between two essentially different – old and new – states of the world but the conflicts emerging within the new state of the world, that is, the modern world. On the one hand, conflicts within civil society, within the bourgeois family, between women and men. On the other hand, conflicts between political powers or institutions such as absolute royal or princely power and republicanism.

In the Enlightenment philosophy and drama do not simply constitute a parallel history, philosophy becomes an active participant and midwife in the birth of modern, non-tragic drama. Philosophers, such as Diderot and Lessing, not only discuss the arts, mainly drama, they were also dramatists themselves, putting their ideas into practice. Conversely, leading dramatists such as Schiller were also engaged in theoretical and philosophical justification of their work. At first the justification and the practice of the new domestic bourgeois drama was at the centre of interest. The increasing support for bourgeois drama went together with the emergence of the new genre of the social novel. The central topic of the new social novel was romantic love, love as passion and sexual love. First in the genre of letter novels, such as Richardson's *Clarissa* or Rousseau's *Nouvelle Heloise*, later as first-person testimonies or as third person narratives as in Goethe's *Werther*, *Wilhelm Meister* and *Elective Affinities*.

As far as pre-revolutionary drama is concerned, Diderot's writings on drama (1757), in part translated by Lessing, stand out. In one respect Diderot stood close to the Platonic heritage. He did not separate the discussion of drama from the discussion of audience, actors, socio-political message and reception, using his own dramas as examples of his aesthetic and political views. (To my mind his dramas have rather a political and social than artistic significance.) Aristotle's view that the heroes of tragedies need to be more elevated than the audience was reinterpreted. When speaking of more elevated characters, Diderot and Lessing argued that Aristotle had not meant queens and kings, that is, persons of higher standing in rank or position but persons of higher moral standing and grandeur. Commoners can be as virtuous as kings, they can be as ready to accomplish eminent deeds, they can be as honourable, as dignified and as significant as any king or prince.

The major problems Diderot and Lessing faced were created by their challenge to the doctrine of the three unities of time, place and action and to the socio-political standing of the heroes of a tragic play. Diderot made the case not just for the possibility but for the superiority of serious drama, dramas where burghers, that is, merchants and craftsmen, occupy the stage and meet their fate as tragic characters. In one important respect Diderot's answer was not entirely satisfactory. Burghers, merchants, craftsmen and artists could be the protagonists of modern domestic drama, they could even act heroically, yet how far could their influence reach? Can they influence the fate of their city, of their times, can they accomplish something great for and in history? After all, in traditional Greek, Renaissance or Baroque tragedies, to be a king or a queen not only signalled their status and rank but also their power to decide for others and influence the fate of their world. Their decisions and actions made a difference for their people, their city and their state. They were not only mirroring an age, they were also changing it. The moment one places bourgeois figures at the centre of the plot, be they as virtuous or as vicious as a king, their fate or action will not influence, even less change their world.

Recognition of the importance of the action radius in a drama was only one of the reasons for the turn with Schiller towards historical drama as an alternative to domestic bourgeois drama. The other reason or rather motivation for turning towards historical drama was the emergence of the idea of historicism. Historicism took root after the French Revolution in the form of the grand narrative of world history – the story of universal progress leading from the remote past to the present that will (or might) continue from the present towards a promising future. The historical development of the world was regarded as a continuum, in which all cultures occupied an important place and were overcome in turn by higher cultures. The grand narrative became a branch of universalism, of a new idea of humankind, in which the world spirit stands, in Hegel's words, above all partial justifications.

As far as universalism is concerned, we need to begin with Kant, for whom humankind dwells in us all as transcendental freedom. Humankind in us is the source of the moral law, of the imperative never to use another human person as mere means but always as an end in itself. In Schiller's *Ode to Joy*, set to music by Beethoven in his Ninth Symphony, we embrace the whole of humankind and kiss the whole world. This spectacle of progressive history was not, however, a fruitful source for drama. Goethe tried it, but the second part of *Faust* was no longer a drama but rather a kind of dramatized poetry.

Goethe and Schiller, the twin stars in the sky of Weimar classicism, created with their reflections on Greek tragedy and culture the cult of ancient Greece on German soil, a cult taken up by German Romanticism (Hölderlin), continued by Hegel and Nietzsche and ending with Heidegger. Being 'classic' meant to follow in the footsteps of the Greeks, yet in both the case of Goethe and Schiller to do so in the spirit of modern universalism and historicism. Goethe's drama *Iphigenia in Tauris* (1786) paid tribute to Greek mythology, and Schiller tried to introduce the chorus in his drama *The Bride of Messina* (1803). However, they were also aware of the historical distance between the ancient Greeks and themselves. In his elegy *The Gods of Greece* Schiller laments the irreversibility of time. The Greek gods are dead, no one fears or believes in them, they are only statues.

To my mind it does not make much sense to distinguish between post-revolutionary enlightenment, classicism and romanticism, since they were combined in varying proportions in the soul and work of different poets. Take for example Hölderlin: according to the historical legend, Hegel, Schelling and Hölderlin together planted a 'tree of liberty' after hearing the news of the French Revolution. Whereas Schiller and Goethe tried to emulate Greek tragedies, Hölderlin translated two plays each of Euripides and Sophocles. He also tried to write three versions of a tragic drama, *The Death of Empedocles* (1797–1800). A philosopher who jumped into the crater of Etna was not an ideal of Greek tragic writers but of a modern one. What attracted Hölderlin to this eccentric rather than tragic figure? On the one hand, republicanism and, on the other hand, adoration for the genius: liberty for the people but also glory for the super-human, god-like man, who reaches the summit! For the moderns love is everywhere. But for Hölderlin the greatest, the most sacred love is not between men and women, not between equals, the greatest love in *Empedocles* is a love between unequals: the glorification of a master by a student and the passionate love of Empedocles for this young and favourite student. This may look Greek, but it is in fact romantic. The language is romantic. The disciples of Socrates did not refer to the passions of their heart and even less did they address their master with words like 'O, Du hoher Mann!' (O high, noble man!). Socrates would never turn to a student, not even to Phaedrus, with words like: 'O Sohn, Sohn meiner Liebe!' (O son, son of my love!). Gadamer believed in the fusion of horizons – theirs and ours, past and present. But, as I see it, there is no such fusion. We are imprisoned in our history or rather in our historical consciousness (even if this is an oxymoron). The emphatic pantheism of Empedocles in Hölderlin's *Trauerspiel* is modern through and through.

The new state of the world, to use again Hegel's expression, made some traditional philosophical ideas about the essence of tragedy problematic. This happened also with the Aristotelian concept of *catharsis*. Instead of being purified of fear and empathy, the audience of domestic bourgeois dramas did what no audience of tragedies ever did, not even in the case of *Hamlet* (*Romeo and Juliet* might have been an exception), they wept. Some domestic dramas were called *comédies larmoyantes* (literally: tearful plays) to distinguish them from tragedies. There remained one option to rescue Aristotle's theory of *catharsis*, namely, to attribute it not to the audience but to one or the other main character within the drama. Catharsis meant then a kind of purification of one's own former self, confessing and becoming another person. This is, of course, more Christian than pagan.

The new (Christian) interpretation of *catharsis* fitted none of the classic Greek dramas – perhaps with the exception of *Oedipus in Colonus*, but it fitted many of Shakespeare's plays: *Lear, Othello, Richard III, Henry IV, Coriolanus*, perhaps also Brutus in *Julius Caesar*. It applied also to some tragedies by Racine, above all to *Phaedra*. In addition, this new understanding of *catharsis* applies to a number of family dramas with burghers as protagonists, such as Ibsen's *A Doll's House* or *Rosmersholm*. To them I will turn later.

Let me return briefly to the years prior to and directly after the French Revolution. Shakespeare was slowly recognized, with the help of Lessing and Goethe, as the greatest and unprecedented tragic author, yet he was not imitated. French writers from Voltaire to Victor Hugo followed a traditional French style with historical plots, national heroes, kingdoms and rulers. However, love – requited and unrequited – was omnipresent. In serious plays as opposed to novels and comedies, love was mostly defeated, for reasons of state or by a tyrannical father, by prejudice, money, position and power. After 'amour passion' was discovered in the 18th century, it soon became the centre of the plot in all genres: in drama, opera, novel, and of course in lyric poetry. The plot could be borrowed from anywhere, from Greek mythology, from Ariosto's *Orlando Furioso*, from episodes and stories in Roman history, from Ovid, Virgil and from the Bible. Yet, whatever the source, love was omnipresent as in Handel's baroque operas. Of course, love and marriage were always a welcome topic in comedy since Plautus and Terence. In Moliere comedy reached a second perfection. A third highpoint was reached in Beaumarchais, whose two Enlightenment comedies of Figaro had a greater social impact than perhaps any comedy before and after. The second, The *Marriage of Figaro* (1778), as adapted by Da Ponte, enabled Mozart to compose in 1786 the best comic opera ever.

Diderot's great theoretical friend, Lessing, the passionate defender of Shakespeare and the enemy of all Aristotelian rules, was also the first who wrote good modern plays with bourgeois protagonists. His best known non-tragic drama or romance, *Nathan the Wise* (1779), is a tale that almost leads to death and devastation but is happily averted by the wisdom of a Jewish sage (Lessing's friend Moses Mendelssohn was the model) and a tolerant Muslim ruler. This is perhaps the first directly philosophical drama, where the plot demonstrates a philosophical theory without preaching. Yet, this was an exception, a non-tragic drama, in which tragedy is avoided not by divine intervention but by human reason.

The work that became the first model for bourgeois domestic drama and opera was Lessing's *Emilia Galotti* (1772). It tells the story of a young girl, who like all pretty young women in a small princedom is easy prey for the ruler. The play ends melodramatically: the daughter asks her father to kill her to save her from seduction by the prince. Contemporaries understood all too well the political message of Emilia's decisive words: 'Violence! Who cannot resist violence! But seduction!' The story, if not the political message, will be a recurring theme in drama and opera alike, from Hugo's *Le roi s'amuse* to Verdi's adaptation of Hugo's play in *Rigoletto*.

Far more complicated is the similar story in one of Schiller's early dramas, *Kabale und Liebe* (Intrigue and Love, 1784), where the young girl, the daughter of a court musician, and the son of the president of the prince fall in love. A kind of Romeo and Juliet story, over-determined by social and class differences, and set like *Emilia Galotti* in a small tyrannical German princedom. The real hero of the play is the girl, a person of great human dignity, whereas the boy is a typical romantic figure, carried away by passions, love, jealousy and irrationality (rather like the poet Tasso in Goethe's play *Torquato Tasso,* 1790). There is another female hero in the drama, a lady of the court, the lover of the prince, at the mercy of her womanizing master, who escapes from the court after the death of the two main protagonists. Before they die the two young lovers, victims of a petty court intrigue, undergo a cathartic experience. Why then can we not call this drama a tragedy? Because it is not the clash of two worlds, of the old and the new, of venerated custom, on the one hand, and free individuality on the other, but the clash between innocence and vice, love and tyranny, freedom and dependency within the same world. This is perhaps the major, constantly recurring conflict within the modern state of the world.

Emilia Galotti (as also two previous plays by Lessing) introduces one of the dominant themes of future dramas: the fate of women. The women characters of domestic drama are unlike the heroines of Greek classic tragedies. Electra, Iphigenia, Antigone and Andromache were passionately committed to a cause, while carrying out the will of a god or a goddess. They were not presenting and representing women's lot (*Medea* by Euripides might be an exception). By contrast, women in the domestic dramas are suffering and defeated because they do not choose their lot: men do it for them and against them (Racine's Phaedra was the first in this long line). They are the bearers of a new conflict, the early heroines of women liberation. Women are not just passionate or sentimental lovers but also the victims of love – not just of the beloved, as anyone can be, but of the world of men. But men too will agonize, fight against love and finally die of love.

Schiller's poetry and plays from beginning to end carry the message of liberty, be it personal (not sexual), social or political. His first drama *Die Räuber* (The Brigands, 1781) earned him recognition and citizenship of the first French Republic in 1792. Schiller was the mouthpiece of the great modern ideas of love, liberty and progress. Some of his heroes, Wilhelm Tell or Don Rodrigo in *Don Carlos* (1787) were freedom fighters, while others, like Don Carlos were early modern romantics like Werther, standing for the freedom of subjectivity and caring for nothing but love and liberty. Schiller's dramas were true dramas. In *Don Carlos* the two great, dominating passions are not burning in one and the same breast but are divided between two very close friends: Rodrigo who lives for liberty, Carlos who lives for love. Why do they both lose everything at the end of the drama? Why do they die? Not because of their dual passions but because of other dual passions, jealousy and fanaticism. Here is not the place to discuss the weaknesses of the drama. Briefly: too many details, too close to historical facts, e.g. the defeat of the Spanish Armada, and too long. Moreover, although Schiller centres the play around the conflict between tyranny and republicanism, he also identifies with republican, liberal ideas and gives one or the other actor long and enthusiastic speeches about the justice of his cause. This is why many of Schiller's dramas are exceedingly rhetorical. Yet, what is a shortcoming in the theatre can be profitable on the opera stage, where rhetoric becomes aria, and the drama concise. In Verdi's *Don Carlos* Schiller's drama becomes a masterpiece.

To return to the end of the 18th century – the age giving birth to the belief in the idea of progress, to revolutionary dreams and the dominance of romantic love: it is a non-tragic age. It is the age introduced by Mozart's *Don Giovanni* (1787), where the old – evil – world perishes. True, grandeur perishes together with it, yet the decent and less decent, romantic and prosaic citizens of a new world happily sing together on the stage they will occupy from now on. We are in a world where the narrow-minded womanizing count loses the game against his witty servant Figaro, a world where the universality of a Sarastro is triumphant, a world where being a man is superior to being a prince and where finally reason rules supreme. We are in Mozart's world.

When Mozart's operas appeared, on the stage of history a king was being guillotined, the cream of French aristocracy lost their lives and power, new institutions were established, and old ones collapsed. After Mozart's death, a new kind of war with a new modern hero entered the historical stage. Napoleon, the self-made man, became the model for the ambitious youth of the coming century. Revolutions, great passions, formidable characters, deadly conflicts, great battles appeared on the historical scene, but where were the tragedies? Where were the contemporary heroes resembling the former tragic heroes? Louis XVI, Robespierre, Napoleon – were they not tragic heroes just like Richard II or Henry VI?

Politics was invented in ancient Athens, so was historiography. Yet, as we saw, political history or historiography (with the exception of *The Persians*) did not become the subject matter for tragedies in Athens or Rome. Roman history first qualified as a subject for drama and occasionally for tragedy in the Renaissance and the Baroque, when opera composers or Shakespeare and later Corneille and Racine were confronted with the dramatic and sometimes tragic conflicts of their own age and the history of their times. Shakespeare was the first to write historical dramas, not only about the Roman past but also about the past of his own present, the War of the Roses. For his great tragic plays like *Hamlet*, *Lear*, *Othello* and *Macbeth* he borrowed quasi-historical stories from chronicles that embodied the clash between two entirely different worlds: the old and the new.

The experience of the rapidly changing historical developments of the 17th to 19th centuries, and the new type of political conflict between monarchy and republic within an already established modernity changed historical consciousness in Europe. The idea of progress, the so called grand narrative emerged and in its wake the idea of universal history, seen in the light of an unstoppable, albeit sometimes halted, progressive development from the simple to the complex, from the primitive to the civilized, from ignorance to the ever growing accumulation of knowledge. It was presumed, first by Condorcet and Lessing, that contemporary conflicts, dramatic conflicts included, are inherent in this universal historical development and that they all express the same historical consciousness. The historicism, born from the new historical consciousness was thoroughly modern; not only did it presuppose a universal history as universal progress, or alternatively, as universal regress, it also made the present part of the universal story. Whether by celebrating or attacking it, the new world became the world of dissatisfaction, the world of Goethe's

Faust, who can never tell the beautiful moment to stay as long as 'captain forward' drives him on. In this respect, enlightenment and romanticism are branches of the same tree of historicism.

Historical novels and historical dramas were also branches of the same tree. The historical novels of Walter Scott were sometimes called romantic because he told the story of the destruction of the Scottish tribes as a kind of loss. Yet, at the same time, he saw the victory of modernity as unavoidable and finally even a fruitful result of this loss. The essential difference between historical novels and historical dramas is not due to differences in their historical consciousness, since this is what they both share. It is rather a compositional requirement, pointed out by Lukács. In the case of historical drama the main characters should be famous historical actors who put their mark on the events of their times: kings and queens, generals and warriors. In historical novels, however, the protagonists should not be taken from history but rather invented. Fictional characters should stand in the centre of the historical conflict, having contact with the main political actors on both sides. The main political actors should appear only in episodes, preferably in one single episode, where their real grandeur or pettiness will be revealed, as with Richard the Lionheart in Scott's *Ivanhoe* or – Lukács's example – Napoleon in Tolstoy's *War and Peace*.

Historical dramas (and occasionally historical short stories) offered opera composers what they need most: strong characters, interrelated deadly political, social and personal conflicts, love, requited and unrequited, friendships, displays of courage, misunderstandings, contingencies, evil intriguers, self-sacrifice, passion and enthusiasm. Real historical characters catch the public's interest, even if the characters are transformed. Modern historical dramas and novels were born in the post-revolutionary age, just as Shakespeare's tragedies came after the War of the Roses. Yet while Shakespeare wrote several tragic dramas about the Wars of the Roses to arrive almost in his own present with *Henry VIII*, very few dramatic works – and no tragedies – were written about the revolutions of 1789–94. The one significant example of a revolutionary drama is *Danton's Death* (1835) by the young Büchner (1813–1837). The author called his brilliant play a drama. Why not a tragedy?

Danton, one of the leaders of one of the political wings of the French revolution, who was responsible for the September prison massacres with many innocent victims, is accused together with a young associate Camille Desmoulins of being an enemy of the revolution. Danton, for all that he is a cynic and hedonist, shows great political courage and conviction, certain that everything he says and has done belongs to the theatre of world history and is destined to go down in history. (He was right.) Büchner was the first to present the revolution as a god who devours his own children, as in Goya's painting of

Cronos. Büchner portrays his trio of protagonists – Danton, Robespierre and Saint Just – as equally significant historical actors, even though he places the spectators on Danton's side. He even suggests (rightly) that as far as history is concerned all the actors stand on the same side. They are all sitting in the same boat on the same river trying to steer the boat in different directions. None of the three historical actors is challenged by an outside historical power from a different world. Even the typical modern political conflict between monarchy and republic is replaced here by a deadly conflict within the republic. (This is also the reason why no tragedy could be written about the victims of the Soviet show trials.)

Büchner ended his historical drama with a great final scene. The half-crazed wife of the executed Camille Desmoulins, Lucie, appears in the crowd applauding the execution and suddenly shouts: 'God save the King!' She is seized and carried away. The missing 'other side' appears at the last moment. Of course, it is not Büchner's shortcoming that the other side is not party to the drama, for the fate of this other side, of absolute monarchy, has already been settled, not in a tragic or perhaps not even in a dramatic way. The monarchy has already left the historical stage, falling like a Greek king from the heights to the depths, from power and glory into nothingness. Unlike Oedipus, Napoleon and his fate will not be subjects of tragedy, however. Not because Napoleon died of natural causes – after all, Oedipus also died of a natural cause (old age) – but because Napoleon was not the representative of a doomed world but the hero of the new world of self-made men and the beginnings of nationalism.

There is, to my knowledge, only one drama that engages with the revolutionary wars as they unfolded. Not directly, but indirectly. I refer to Schiller's trilogy about the Thirty Years War: *Wallenstein's Camp* (1798), *The Two Piccolomini* (1799) and *Wallenstein's Death* (1799). This is the sole drama Schiller modelled on Greek tragedies as three plays in historical sequence. Reading the trilogy one can easily detect the essential differences between Shakespeare's historical plays and those in the age of historicism. I mention only two. Who is the traitor? It is easy to answer this question in Shakespeare, yet difficult in the case of Schiller. To whom should one be loyal in Shakespeare? To friends, family, tribe, oath of allegiance or the master? When Aenobarbus, the friend and general of Mark Anthony, betrays him by joining Caesar, not just we (the spectators) despise him as a traitor, he also despises himself. In Schiller's trilogy, however, there is no cause or commitment of which anyone could say that this is the 'right' one.

The Wallenstein trilogy places the viewers in the time of the Thirty Years War, more precisely in the fifteenth year of this war. Wallenstein is a commander on the Catholic side. At one point he asks himself if the war is justified? Is not Europe and the peace of Europe more important than gaining a little additional territory for the Austrian Catholic Emperor? (I think that this is the first time in a historical drama that Europe's wellbeing appears as value, as a cause.) Wallenstein turns to the Protestant Swedish army. Is he a traitor? A traitor for what and to whom? He states that his understanding with the Swedish general is a means to the goal of bringing an end to this terrible war that is leaving Europe devastated. He is a traitor to the Austrian Emperor, for sure, but is he a traitor to the Catholic side as well? Is not peace desirable also for them?

This depends on the audience of 1800, whether Protestant, Catholic, or pacifist, when the complete drama was first staged, at the time of the first Napoleonic wars. An urgent question is asked of Schiller's German audience. Is the Austrian Emperor worth defending, is it right to shed the blood of our compatriots fighting against the French self-made man? Some from the audience would have answered in the affirmative: the virtue of loyalty stands above all other justifications. Wallenstein could have refused the honour of leading the Catholic army, but now that he has accepted it, he is duty bound to stand by his own choice. Others could have sided with Wallenstein, accepting his argument that if one has to choose between two wrongs, one should choose the lesser wrong.

The other novelty in the Wallenstein drama is the generational conflict between the two Piccolomini: Octavio the father and Max his son. They love one another. Their conflict develops over a cause and in connection with the cause over political morality. Kant, Schiller's philosophical master, wrote an essay about political morality, the spirit of which Schiller follows in creating the character of Max Piccolomini. There is, however, one actor in the drama, whom, at the end the play, the audience unanimously rejects: the father Octavio, who organizes the murder of Wallenstein and accepts the reward from the Austrian Emperor – the title of prince.

2   Drama and Classical German Philosophy

Historical drama and bourgeois drama on the one hand, the idealization of the Greeks on the other, characterized the German-speaking theatre in the years from Kant to Hegel and Beethoven. In terms of my parallel history the question I want to ask is whether there is an intimate relation between the development of early modern German non-tragic drama and the development of classical German philosophy. I mentioned already one common inspiration: historical thinking. The grand narrative of the idea of a universal history of progress formed the golden thread of all classical German philosophers up to 1830 at least. The most representative aspect of this idea of development is *dialectics*.

Since its conception philosophical thinking has taken inspiration from negation. The empirical reality was negated by a transcendental idea: what is generally believed to be good, beautiful and true is neither good nor beautiful nor true. Something else is good, beautiful and true and this something is grasped by true knowledge. Empirical opinion and transcendental knowledge collided first in dialogue form. Plato wanted to be a tragic poet, but under the influence of Socrates he became the first philosophical writer. He formulated his philosophy in non-tragic dialogues. The dialogues were non-tragic, since the participants of Plato's philosophical dialogues did not position themselves in relation to the old time and the new time but took contradictory viewpoints in understanding and judging the same time. The empirical world, i.e. how people normally live, see and judge their own time, is radically rejected as a world of appearance when confronted with the transcendental world, the world of ideas, the true world. The confrontation between these two worlds, these two positions develops in Plato through dialogue. Opposed views of the two worlds are presented and voiced by characters. Socrates represents the position of the true, transcendental, world. The position of some participants changes under the spell or influence of Socrates' questions. Dialectics first appears as the confrontation of two fundamental positions within the same world. Philosophical conflicts after Plato rarely take a similarly dramatic form. They are normally replaced by the confrontation of different arguments, by refutation and confirmation. Most philosophical systems do not even present the empirical standpoint in order to refute it. If a system starts, for example, with the definition of *causa sui* as in Spinoza's *Ethics* this is obvious. In the case of Descartes, it is less obvious. He begins his *Discourse on Method* with the story of his pre-philosophical personal experience. But once he arrives at ego cogito, the empirical world immediately disappears.

All philosophical systems, whatever their method, are open to four kinds of reception. The first kind I call *total* reception. I mean the case when a philosopher embraces or rejects another philosophy as a whole. Doubtless every understanding is a misunderstanding, and there are no two identical total receptions. The other three kinds consist of *partial* receptions, where philosophies are interpreted to answer only one question among Kant's three questions: what can I know, what should I do, and how might –should – I live. This last question is broader than Kant's: what might I hope. One conclusion we can immediately draw from the answer to the third question. This kind of reception of a philosophy as guidance for our way of life is never tragic. It can be stoic, epicurean, sceptic, religious – but never tragic. Even the reception of Schopenhauer's pessimistic philosophy was not tragic. His pessimistic portrayal of the human condition worked rather as a kind of consolation in cases of depression or despair, as for Thomas Buddenbrooks in Thomas Mann's novel.

It is only after the French Revolution, in Kant's three Critiques from the 1790s, that dialectics occupied again a central position.

Let me start with the First Critique, second part, the dialectics of pure reason. (I will not of course introduce, even less interpret Kant's position and arguments as I have elsewhere. I shall emphasize only his conceptions relevant to our parallel history.) Before discussing the cases of the dialectics of pure reason Kant introduces the concept of the transcendental idea, distinguishing it from Plato's *idea* by confessing his commitment to the modern age. The supreme idea of human freedom, he says, is freedom represented by the moral law, since the freedom of one man presupposes the freedom of all.

In the presentation of the dialectics of cosmological ideas, Kant replays in one respect the old discussion between Callicles and Socrates, where both discussion partners could equally well prove the truth of their opposed arguments. In Plato's world, however, one statement is mere opinion and the other is true, thus the two statements have no equal worth and no equal theoretical weight. In Kant, however, all contradicting statements are antinomies, that is, both are true. One is true from the empirical position, the other from the transcendental position. Kant, unlike Plato, does not divide the two standpoints between two characters of a dialogue, but undertakes the process of argumentation in both cases. He stands behind both arguments, thus demonstrating their equal correctness. His solution to the contradiction is the statement that A is true from the transcendental, whereas B is true from an empirical standpoint. To simplify the matter, I would say that Kant started to occupy a perspectivist standpoint at least in the presentation of the dialectic in the *Critique of Practical Reason*, when he drew attention to a very modern problem, to the contradiction between freedom (including pure practical reason) and happiness – a contradiction unheard of not just in antiquity but also in the mediaeval period and early modernity (Descartes or Spinoza). Happiness is, says Kant, subjective, it has no unfailing objective criteria, it has more to do with feelings, perhaps even with contingency. In contrast, says Kant, freedom does have objective criteria. This is a modern philosophical suggestion, not even necessarily connected to the priority of practical reason in Kant. The old question: when was Oedipus happy? When he was an adored as a king or in Colonus? The ancient philosophers said, in Colonus, because he had gained knowledge. Kant would have said, since happiness is subjective, that he was happier as a king yet more worthy of happiness in Colonus.

Let us go back now to early modern drama from *Emilia Galotti* to Schiller's historical dramas or even to Goethe's *Tasso*. The choices between freedom, moral and personal, and happiness are mostly in collision, either between two or more actors or within the soul of the one actor. There are characters whose overwhelming passion is freedom. In their soul there is no conflict between morality and happiness – if there is no moral and political freedom, there can be no happiness (the Marquis of Posa in Schiller's *Don Carlos*). There are characters, like Don Carlos, whose main passion is love, for whom freedom is secondary. There is no happiness for Max Piccolomini without Tekla, yet he makes a free moral choice that leads him to sacrifice happiness and life. Neither Hamlet nor Lear – not even a main character in Shakespeare's comedies – has to choose between freedom and happiness, and even if there is such a collision, there is no conflict between of freedom and happiness within their souls. The same can be said about the main characters in Corneille and Racine. 19th century opera, however, will draw inspiration exactly from this conflict.

Kant addresses philosophical questions in a new way, in the spirit of his time, yet still as a fully rounded conclusive philosophy. Drama writers could not do the same when devising characters and plots. It became obvious to them too that consensus concerning the main virtues and values, especially the understanding and judging of these virtues and values, had been lost. The Christian world had modified the value system of the ancient world; new virtues and vices such as humility versus pride were added to the ancient virtues of courage, temperance, justice and wisdom. Nevertheless, the value system remained consensual and stable. Philosophers from Spinoza onwards detected the loss of both consensus and stability in the modern age, but they only modified the old system by maintaining – like Spinoza – wisdom (knowledge of the third degree and in ethics adequate knowledge) at the top of the value hierarchy while other philosophers rather avoided the question.

Hume addressed the new situation in his own way. He did not discuss moral action and the criteria of moral action since, according to him, action is motivated and ought to be motivated not by reason but by passions. He rather took the standpoint of judgment, as in aesthetics. Just as the aesthetic question is addressed with reference to the judgment of taste, so the moral question is to be addressed with reference to moral judgment. In both cases moral value or worth is decided by the judgment of the recipients. This solution was possible for Hume, since he could still presuppose a kind of moral consensus in his social world. Not as a *consensus omnium* to be sure, since his idea of consensus was far from being universalist but rather that of a society and a culture shared by actors and recipients alike (e.g. the British society of gentlemen).

In Hume's mind there is a natural virtue common to all and this is sympathy. We feel sympathy for those close to us, similar to us and in close contact to us. On this ground he replaces the traditional pairing of fundamentally opposite passions like love and hatred or attraction and repulsion by the pair pride and shame. Pride and shame as basic passions presuppose a community of judgment. If within the same society one person is ashamed whereas another rather proud of doing or approving the same thing, Hume's recipe could not work. I may add that when it comes to the understanding of certain virtues, and especially the virtue of justice, Hume's approach is as sound and as relevant at present as it was in his day. For instance, when speaking about distributive justice, Hume observed that the value or virtue of justice can be validated only in a world of relative scarcity like ours, since justice is invalid under the conditions of absolute scarcity and superfluous under the condition of abundance.

Kant, who respected both Hume and Rousseau, took a position that unified three great modern ideas: freedom, universality and individuality. His moral philosophy presupposed first that individuals are potentially autonomous moral actors, that each and every individual decides on his own his action in every situation. Second, that the decisions of an individual are moral only if the decision (act) is standing for universality, that is, normative for humankind. Third, the decision is free only if it is determined by transcendental freedom alone (the 'alone' is important). Such a moral act is possible if the individual, before embarking on an action (choice), asks whether the maxim of his action qualifies for universal legislation. The actor should ask himself whether he could wish that every human being should act likewise under the guidance of this maxim. Thus, if you decide that in a special situation it would be better for you (and perhaps also for others) to lie, you are morally lost, even if the consequences of your choice are beneficial. By lying, whatever the circumstances, you introduce a lie into the world. If anyone in any situation were permitted to lie, the distinction between lying and telling the truth would disappear from the world.

Kant's demonstration is far more complicated, but it was mainly understood in this way. Writers, especially dramatists, fought against his moral absolutism or confirmed it. I mentioned already that Schiller fought against it. A drama that confirmed it was *The Prince of Homburg* (1810) by Kleist. The drama was written shortly before the suicide of its author, who knew Kant's works on morality. According to Kant's moral philosophy, suicide was an act against the moral law. Was Kleist thinking about this when he upheld Kant's rigorous theory in his last drama? The young Prince of Homburg, the hero of the drama, is a kind of romantic youth, like Goethe's Tasso, ambitious, dreaming of military glory, in love with the niece of the Prince Elector, in whose army he fights.

Disobeying the command of the Prince Elector he attacks the enemy and wins the battle of Fehrbellin. Because of disobeying his command, he is condemned to death. He despairs and begs for clemency. Finally, the Prince Elector decides that he will pardon him under the condition that he (the Prince of Homburg) prove that the punishment was unjust. The young Prince begins his Kantian ruminations. He won the battle, and this was the consequence of his disobedience, but does a good consequence make the punishment unjust? If I disobey a command and introduce disobedience into the world, neither command nor obedience will be left. Thus, he comes to the Kantian conclusion that the punishment, the death sentence, is just. He declares that he is ready to die, for the judgment was just, since he cannot prove the opposite. Even the end of the drama is Kantian. The Prince is taken to the place of execution, blindfolded, waiting to be shot. But who awakes him from his swoon? Not the angel of death but his beloved, who places the laurel wreath of victory on his head. The virtuous deserve happiness! The Prince attains the goal of his dreams.

According to Hegel the subjectivity of antinomies was Kant's shortcoming. Dialectics for Hegel was objective. This means (again to simplify) that difference and contradiction are inherent in things themselves. Whether in the realm of 'subjective spirit' (subjective personal understanding, knowledge), or in the realm of 'objective spirit' (the history of societies, states, cultures), or in the realm of 'absolute spirit' (the history of art, religion, philosophy) the same kind of development takes place. Differences (within personal knowledge, historical period, art, religion and philosophy) develop into contraries, contraries into contradiction, and finally knowledge, such that things, periods, etc. become their own 'other.' The same happens with this other, since it will also be negated, the opposites are then reconciled on a higher level – and so the development continues. Although the frequently quoted triad 'thesis-antithesis-synthesis' stems from Schelling and not from Hegel, Hegel's understanding of self-development is generally understood in this simplified way. What was most important for Hegel and – critically – also for post-Hegelians, was that the end result of all the developments in their totality will become a system that closes the (hi)story. Why is this so important for Hegel? Because only in this way could metaphysics, that is, traditional philosophy, be rescued, and rescuing philosophy meant rescuing the self-consciousness and the self-knowledge of European history.

For Hegel philosophy is our world grasped in concepts. What happens to a world that is no longer grasped in concepts? Obviously, it loses self-consciousness. Yet, why is philosophy identical with metaphysical systems? Above all, why is the end of philosophy, a century and a half after the end of its older sister tragedy, also the end of history, the end of religion, the end of art? Why are we left with a world painted grey in grey? Why in short does Hegel declare the end of Europe just as Aristotle did of Athens?

Before trying to answer these questions so many have tried to answer, two things need to be clarified. First: the grand narrative from Lessing, Condorcet and Kant to Marx was told – and is still told (where it is told) – from the standpoint of European modernity. It is never told of anywhere else, not even of the USA. Can this story still be told, now that the whole world with its entirely different histories has become modern? Didn't the story end at the very point Hegel ended it? Second: why could metaphysics be rescued only by turning it into history? And why is the end of metaphysics the end of history? An equation that was confirmed, even if challenged, by many significant post-Hegelians, from Marx and Kierkegaard up to Heidegger? Were they right?

The second question looks easier to answer. Traditional metaphysics looked like a building. Sensation, perception, passions etc. normally occupied the ground floor, ordinary thinking, beliefs, identity logic, praxis, *techné*, scientific knowledge, causality, virtues the first and the second floor, Sophia (wisdom), Reason, Truth the highest floor and in the tower dwelled the Sun, the Pure Forms and God. The building was modified, but it remained a building built from the low towards the high, from the impure to the pure, mostly distinguishing from Plato onwards through to Descartes, Spinoza, Leibniz and even Hobbes essence from appearance, substance from attributes.

When was this metaphysical building first undermined or abandoned? Hume led the way. The metaphysical edifice, like all social and political hierarchies, was rendered suspect by one single sentence: 'all humans are born equally free.' Kant, the first to recognize the challenge, wanted to rescue philosophy while remaining entirely on the ground of the Enlightenment. The critical system served his goal. Kant realized that without distinguishing between the transcendental and the empirical level of thinking there is no philosophy, and that giving up knowledge of the transcendent is worth the sacrifice for the preservation of the transcendental. However, even if Kant's starting point, the faculties of the mind, no longer resemble the image of a building, the strict division between low and high, between impure and pure reconfirms it.

Hegel claimed not to be an architect, aiming at creating an architectonical system, as Kant did, but aiming rather to tell one great unified story, the story of our world. In fact, he told several stories, finally putting them all together in the grand story of the Whole. All the partial stories develop dialectically to finally arrive at Totality. The grand story (a kind of historical, temporalized Spinozism) does not guide us from the low to the high but from the simple to the complex, contrary to Christian metaphysics, where the simple (God) is the highest since it is totally homogeneous and unchanging. The stories are all told by Hegel from the position of their result and end in the present, since no story can be told other than from its end and the end of world history is the present. The story of development is told from the highest standpoint, the story of the parts from the standpoint of the whole, the totality – just as it always was in all metaphysical buildings, where the end result is presupposed already in the first sentence. The difference lies solely in the difference between argumentation and storytelling.

World history, the story of objective spirit that leads to modernity begins with oriental cultures, Chinese, Indian, Mesopotamian, then Jewish (seen with European-Lutheran eyes) It is already obvious that world history is told from the position of modern Europeans and Hegel's time. World history is from Condorcet onwards the self-consciousness of post-Enlightenment European culture.

There are at least two aspects where Hegel confronts us with a new interpretation of the story. First: in the preceding grand narratives, the development of scientific knowledge and of technology determines or at least triggers the progress of all other factors. In Hegel, however, the yardstick to measure progress is not the accumulation of scientific knowledge and technology. Knowledge surely accumulates but the real accumulation is philosophical not technical, it is the self-consciousness of the whole dynamism of development, that is, of history, culminating in absolute knowing. Even the question whether this historical development is progressive is not easy to answer. Modernity (politically speaking constitutional monarchy, sociologically speaking heterogeneous civil society) is more 'progressive' than earlier phases of historical development, since 'freedom for all' offers better and greater options for human actors. Yet, there are, according to Hegel, also considerable losses. The modern world becomes prosaic, an underclass is constantly reproduced and religious congregations are disappearing. There are gains and losses, not just gains.

If the development of scientific knowledge (know what and know how) is not the motor of history, what is then its motor? It is certainly not philosophy but rather for Hegel the World Spirit. What is this mysterious World Spirit? A kind of deity? God in History? The development of Hegel's World Spirit is often compared to the development of a single person. First comes childhood, then young adulthood, finally ripe old age. Hegel also suggests this comparison. For my part I think that Hegel's model was rather the self-development of spiritual production, mainly but not solely in philosophy. A philosopher (Plato) comes up with an answer to a problem, the next (Aristotle) falsifies the first position and comes up with another answer. Many thinkers of the Middle Ages take such syntheses as a starting point for a new Christian version. In his lectures on the history of philosophy Hegel tells exactly this story. No philosophy has given an entirely incorrect answer, none of them was entirely misguided, there is some truth and some untruth in all of them. All of them together constitute The Truth, since absolute knowledge cannot be negated. The Whole is the Truth. All the rivers in Hegel's grand narrative end in the same Ocean.

Let me cast a brief glance at the philosophy of art. At first the form of a work exceeds its content (Oriental art), next, form and content are in harmony (Greek and Roman art), finally the content exceeds the form (modern, romantic art). There are also sub-trinities within each and every stage. As we can see, Hegel works through the historical sequence of art's development that has ended in the present. There can be new works of art, but they cannot come up with a new combination of content and form, since the possible combinations have already been exhausted. All future artworks will just reproduce and imitate or write, compose, paint endless variations of the already performed, written and painted.

Wherever one looks at world history from the history of societies, of state forms, of different kinds of social hierarchies to histories of art, religion or philosophy: all the possibilities have been exhausted in the history of European culture in the broadest meaning of the word. The heroes of history like Alexander, Julius Caesar and Napoleon promoted the next new formation of the World Spirit, the new message, the new challenge for the people of Europe and the world. They were great because they helped the forward march of World History. What can happen now that History has ended and there is no next step to be taken or promoted and there is no longer place for great progressive historical heroes, only for sham heroes, for caricatures? What had been once a tragedy can be repeated only as a comedy. No one will guide us to leap into another, new, perhaps better future. The modern world is comic.

This short recourse to Kant and Hegel was not a mere excursus in my history. To repeat Hegel's dictum: philosophy is the age of the philosopher expressed in concepts. In order to continue my parallel history I have to ask the Hegelian question: what kind of spirit of their times did drama embody? In the case of Kant, I have already referred to Schiller and Kleist. Did Hegel's contemporaries share the same spirit that he claimed to have expressed in concepts? What about Hegel in relation to literature and especially drama during the first half of the 19th century?

For Hegel everything develops from the abstract towards the concrete, that is, it will contain more and more 'determinations' and become more complex. This development characterizes drama after the French Revolution. Before the Enlightenment, neither the characters nor the plots of tragedies were invented by the authors. The audience knew them already. The authors did change details to present the plot and the characters in a new light but not the fundamental story. This is why Diderot could say that comedy writers need more genius since they invent the plot and the characters. This changed entirely in the Enlightenment. Non-historical, merely invented characters appeared on the stage in almost all bourgeois dramas. The plot of *Emilia Galotti* or of *Minna von Barnhelm* (1767) was invented by Lessing. The author chose his material freely. This is, to a degree, also the case when dramatists chose stories from history. Why did Goethe choose Egmont, Schiller Wilhelm Tell or Mary Stuart? Figures that were not traditional and had nothing to do with German history? The drama itself, that is, the characters and the plot, had to justify these choices. Plots became complex and their development was usually also unexpected. There are fewer monologues in which characters disclose their motives to us or even to another actor: hence, more guesswork, more complications and sometimes over-complications. The dramatist presents too many aspects, such as several possible motivations for a deed or a decision. It is rarely clear even for the character what and why s/he chooses. It is sometimes also unclear why the losers lose. It is scarcely ever because of a fatal mistake. Schiller's heroine in *Maria Stuart* (1800) committed crimes but they did not seal her fate. The spectator or reader has to decide whether Schiller's Wallenstein committed a mistake. History and historical circumstances are the major players in bourgeois domestic dramas just as much as in historical dramas. History can operate behind the back of the actors replacing tragic fate (although history is not identical with fate). All the actors are part of the movement of history that plays a major role in their various fates. They have not grasped the cunning of the world spirit working behind their back.

After the great Revolution, after the Napoleonic wars, the world of reason turned out finally to be the world of the bourgeoisie, that is, Hegel's prosaic, non- heroic world. There remained no place for great deeds, no fertile ground for tragedy or even serious drama. Nostalgia for tragedy replaced tragedy either as a longing for the rebirth of tragedy or as vain attempts to write tragedies. However, nostalgia for grandeur was not the whole story. We have arrived in the post-Hegelian world of the novel and opera. And, parallel to it, the world of radical philosophy.

3   Modern Drama and Radical Philosophy

No other philosophies influenced drama to the extent that radical philosophy did, the philosophy of Marx, Kierkegaard, Nietzsche and Freud, both in their lifetime but above all later. To speak in Hegel's terms: the tired, exhausted world spirit appears in radical philosophies in the form of negation. They negated the Hegelian system, metaphysics, their own times, the 'present world' (Kierkegaard). In Marx and Nietzsche a kind of affirmation is the answer to negation: affirmation of a world-to-come, including an anthropological turn. Marx and Nietzsche cannot accept Hegel's dictum about the end of history. They make a case for hope, like Nietzsche, or for hope under the mask of certainty, like Marx. For Kierkegaard and Freud, however, no radically new world or radically new man appears on the historical-philosophical horizon.

Prior to the radical philosophers, two minor thinkers had already detected the 'turn' and reacted to it, Feuerbach and Schopenhauer. Both influenced radical philosophers more or less intimately and both were soon abandoned. I could perhaps add to the list Schelling's late positive philosophy as well. Both Feuerbach and Schopenhauer were critics of Hegel, Schopenhauer even his personal enemy. Yet, they could not be more different. Schopenhauer relied on Kant, although he transformed the Kantian system in several essential aspects, among others by replacing transcendental Freedom by the Will. Schopenhauer's pessimistic philosophy was welcome in the post-revolutionary world of lost illusions and the cultivation of 'elegant' sickness. Feuerbach swept away Hegel's rationalism, his emphasis on logic and everything spiritual to the neglect of the real, sensuous person of flesh and blood. Human essence, says Feuerbach, dwells in all human beings but it has been alienated and placed above them, so that humans worship their own alienated essence as God. Feuerbach thus introduced modern atheism, which was more sophisticated than the old vulgar version. He did not attribute religion to the tricks of the priests and admitted the possibility of a religion of subjectivity. Schopenhauer also treated religion with hostility as the source of false hopes and promises, making no concessions to spiritual universality. Within the process of the dissolution of the Hegelian system and metaphysics in general, religion became the first sacrificial lamb chosen by all the radical philosophers. For Marx religion was the opiate of the masses, for Nietzsche it was the fruit of Platonism, the realm of the ascetic priest, and for Freud it was an illusion. Kierkegaard alone took a different position: he attacked the Christianity of his time as a fake and an opiate, to which he opposed true faith, the faith of subjectivity, based on the fundamental paradox of the eternal truth that came into the world historically.

Post-metaphysical philosophy is still philosophy. All the radical philosophers and their two predecessors distinguished between empirical and transcendental levels of discourse, and thus practiced one essential language game of philosophy. Marx and Freud repudiated the name of philosopher, because they believed that only science can lay claim to truth. This is not the place to discuss their claims. One thing, however, can be said: it was not to their scientific discoveries that they owe their lasting influence but to their philosophy.

Something happened during these decades to philosophy that happened perhaps only previously with the stoics, epicureans, and sceptics. The reception of radical philosophers was not mainly philosophical, it extended to a far broader audience. Radical philosophies went beyond models for disciples or admirers, since they offered approaches that all kinds of people could rely upon in acting or in the conduct of life. Their ideas could be and were used as ideologies, as 'isms' (Marxism, existentialism, Freudianism) to justify actions or choices. Their conceptions, promises and interpretations became 'intelligent' topics of conversation. Drama also participated in such discussions. Plays became links in the chain of radical philosophical ideas: Feuerbach and Schopenhauer for Wagner, Marx for Gorky and Brecht, Freud for Eugene O'Neill, Nietzsche for Shaw, Kierkegaard for Ibsen, to mention only a few. One additional 'ism' was not directly philosophical: Darwinism.

In the post-revolutionary years, particularly after 1830, opera became the dominating form of drama. Although both opera composers and dramatists addressed directly or indirectly social and political conflicts of their age, most of them were far from being radical. They did not negate or want to overcome modern bourgeois society. They rather rejected the remnants of the old regime, especially tyranny, conspiracy, abuse of power, prejudices and the like, just as earlier Lessing or Schiller had. Although the popular dramatists of the time (Scribe or Dumas the younger) are, in my view at least, below the level of theoretical significance, we cannot ignore them because 19th century opera had its own parallel history: operas deeply influenced by radical philosophy and those that were not influenced at all. However, the operas without philosophy represented the spirit of their times as much as the dramas of philosophical aspiration. They set to music two dominating ideas of the 19th century: liberty and love. Enthusiasm, empathy, sadness and elevation – opera played on the whole gamut of human emotions. The plot was the foundation, but the real, the main effect was the work of the music, above all the human voice. It carried the message in the choruses and in the arias, which were sung on the street, especially in Italy, by people who had never been to an opera.

The first great operas appeared in Italy in the Renaissance. Although the stories of Monteverdi's operas were traditional (Homer, Roman history), his music initiated a new genre and tradition. In France operas were composed by Lully and Rameau, in England and on German soil by Handel and Gluck. Opera reached its first and highest peak with Mozart – mainly in the comic genre. Nevertheless, opera remained Italian; even in Paris or Vienna operas were sung in Italian. Between 1810 and 1830 with Rossini, Bellini and Donizetti, Italian opera went through a second renaissance musically and also as far as the dramatic plot was concerned. Stories were now borrowed from contemporary sources (e.g. the novels of Walter Scott or dramas of the time), or from European classics like Shakespeare. Whenever tragedies were set to music opera changed them into non-tragic dramas, injecting a dose of operatic melodrama.

Verdi (1813–1901) is the central figure. His operas have remained in the repertoire of opera houses since their first successes. Divas make their name by singing Verdi arias. The audience weeps at the sad end when the lovers lose each other or meet their death. Without the music we would not weep. Verdi's operas are not philosophical. They are political. Nowadays audiences do not always grasp the political message that Italians grasped in Verdi's time, the age of Garibaldi's wars and of the Risorgimento, of the unification of Italian states, of constitutional battles and republican fervour. When listening to the lamentation of the Jews in Babylon in *Nabucco* (1842), we hear Italian men and women singing of their longing for a liberator to come. With *Il Trovatore* (1853) we do not need to know that according to the gossip of Verdi's times, the first king of united Italy, Vittorio Emanuele, was a changeling, the son of a peasant woman. We just understand that Azucena is an Italian peasant woman mistreated by a count, whose son (a changeling) fights like Garibaldi against the tyrannical count. All the melodramatic motives are combined in the plot: love (filial, maternal and sexual), tyranny, the power of song, prejudice, the fight for freedom, and a kind of late remorse (not *catharsis*). There is also 'bourgeois' drama by Verdi, with a similarly fashionable plot: the kept woman who sacrifices herself for love and dies of tuberculosis, a really sad but not tragic story, *La Traviata* (1853, after the younger Dumas). The music and the melodies make us forget Verdi's melodrama and the sometimes poor libretti, even the elephants in *Aida*.

Among the many Verdi operas there are real dramas, where the story provides the opportunity for great music. I mention only two of them. *Don Carlos* (1867) improves on Schiller's drama. The rhetoric of some of the characters (the Marquis of Posa) is transformed in and by song. The drama becomes denser, the relations among the characters simpler and clearer. In turn *The Force of Destiny* (1862) stands very close, as the title suggests, to ancient tragedy. It is, however, a Christian opera, a religious opera, in which there is drama without melodrama. At the time that Italian opera achieved perhaps its summit in Verdi, another kind of opera appeared on the European stage. I refer of course to Wagner (1813–1883) and his music dramas. It is difficult to imagine a greater contrast. Verdi was a kind of naïve artist; Wagner was a theorist who put on stage his own invention: music drama. Verdi felt at home in his time. Wagner was a radical, who began as a revolutionary in politics and remained a revolutionary in music.

Nothing can be more different than the history of Italian and of German opera. Opera was born in Italy and its development was continuous. Thus the renewal of Italian opera at the beginning of the 19th century was only partial just as the essence of Italian opera remained the same after Verdi in *verismo* (Mascagni, Leoncavallo) and in Puccini, even if Puccini was more modern musically and in his libretti, which were taken mostly from everyday life. Let me just add that two of his operas are great dramas. *Tosca* (1900) is a significant modern drama, closer to the tradition of the historical novel than of historical drama. Its main characters are not historical figures but ordinary people, who become heroic without being heroic, out of sheer human decency. Love for a man, love of liberty, solidarity, and self-respect in a situation that is not the result of their character but is imposed from outside. In *The Metaphysics of Tragedy* (1910) Lukács said that tragic heroes are already dead when they appear on the scene. The characters of *Tosca* are not. Perhaps Aristotle's criteria are more appropriate. Tosca, the actress, is a good and loving person but she has one character deficit, jealousy, and because of it that she commits the fatal mistake that will lead to her doom and the doom of her beloved painter. The second significant drama by Puccini is *Turandot* (1924). Here Puccini follows Wagner: he turned from the conflicts of his time and from history to the legendary. *Turandot* belongs to the genre of a romance very much in the Shakespearian tradition.

As opposed to Italian opera the development of German opera was discontinuous. There is no continuity between Gluck and Mozart or between Mozart and Wagner other than the importance and the excellence of the opera texts. There will be no continuity after Wagner either, not even with Richard Strauss. Wagner was not only a composer and writer but also the theorist and interpreter of his own work. In *Opera and Drama* (1852) he contrasted his idea of music drama with the opera of his age. He saw in Rossini the corrupter of the opera tradition. From Rossini on it is the singer who dictates to the composer and the composer to the librettist. The libretto has to serve the composer and above all the singer. The melody of an aria is now the purpose of an opera. This has nothing to do with the essence of drama or of music.

Due to his reading of Feuerbach's *Principles of the Philosophy of the Future* (1843) and *The Essence of Christianity* (1841) and also to his friendly relations with the anarchist Bakunin, Wagner was committed to overcoming through revolution bourgeois society, capitalism, the rule of prose and of mediocrity. For Wagner the greatest sin of the modern world is its hostility to art, of which contemporary opera is one manifestation. He compares the absolute rule of the aria to absolute monarchy. Despite the changes to his political position and his theoretical turn from Feuerbach to Schopenhauer, his hostility against the corrupters of music and drama in the service of the taste of the crowd remained with him to the end. The term 'general or total artwork' (*Gesamtkunstwerk*) did not stem from Wagner. However, it described well the new path that Wagner's work initiated. The drama texts that Wagner wrote were not simply means to serve the music that controlled or governed it, on the contrary drama and music were for him inseparable. When Wagner wrote his dramas, he heard the music, and so do we when reading his dramas. Drama and music together express not only the feelings and thoughts of the characters but also something 'eternal.'

In the case of Mozart, a spontaneous genius, we have little idea about his interpretation of his own operas, whereas we do have Wagner's own interpretations. All the same, audiences understand his characters and their stories in ways that are sometimes essentially differently from Wagner himself. This Wagner knew and wanted. This is why after *Rienzi* (1840) he chose mythological, legendary and not historical figures for his dramas. He wanted to achieve a practically infinite interpretability through the choice of the topic of the drama. No historical background needed to be provided and no complicated psychology was needed to explain the motivations of characters. The legendary plots could be as evident as the Greek tragedies. Now that interpretation through the staging is more important than arias in the presentation of an opera, Wagner's music dramas have become the preferred victims of re-interpretation. This is also why the young Nietzsche could discover and welcome in Wagner's work the rebirth of tragedy. Wagner himself never termed his music dramas tragedies, even though Siegfried's story, in the first Feuerbachian version of the *Ring* cycle, might have qualified as tragedy.

The will to tragedy was first voiced by the young Nietzsche under the impact and influence of Wagner. It was widely shared before the First World War as for example in Lukács's *The Metaphysics of Tragedy*. There was no will to tragedy in Wagner, however, not even in the *Ring* cycle, even though it was bringing back at least one aspect of the typical tragic situation: the demise of the old world, the great spectacle of the world of the gods. The madman in Nietzsche's *Gay Science* (1882) who runs to the marketplace shouting, 'God is dead!' spelled out something sensed by thinkers across the century. Schiller wrote a poem about the end of the gods of Greece, Hegel recalled the cry over the sea 'the great Pan is dead'; in a less poetic vein, he talked about the end of religion. Heine, who was respected by Nietzsche, said that when we go to church we pay tribute to a dead God.

The ideas tragic heroes and heroines believed in and fought for are always related to something they considered to be sacred, values beyond the scope of individual choice. Whether these sacred values involved defence of the dignity of one's family, of tradition, of religion, or the right or even the obligation to revenge crimes personally (natural for Hamlet, absurd for Ottavio in *Don Giovanni*), it was always something one believed in unconditionally, something one was ready to live and to die for. After the 'death of God,' of the 'sacred,' however, all this sounded extravagant, overplayed and even bombastic. The poet, especially the dramatist, in search of his characters, had to turn either to the empirical, that is, the prosaic reality of the times, or to break with it and construct a world with characters of faith and grandeur on a stage set for transcendental souls in the heaven of art, that is, for tragedy.

Wagner appeared before the madman's cry 'God is dead' sounded, although he already sensed it. Interpreters keep asking the question whether *Lohengrin*, *Tannhäuser* or *Parsifal* are religious works, whether they corroborate Christian faith or challenge it. In the case of *Tannhauser* ((1845), a 'romantic opera' as Wagner called it, and *Lohengrin* (1850), the question is marginal, in *Parsifal* (1882), however, it becomes central. The same question was also asked about Kierkegaard. Did Kierkegaard defend Christian faith or challenge it? One may say that he confirmed it in that he reconfirmed Augustine's thesis that truth could be not be grasped internally through recollection (Socrates) but only through God's grace. But one can also say that Kierkegaard challenged Christianity when he stated that there are no Christians left. Everyone is pagan, indeed, worse than pagan, since they do not know it.

The questions whether *Parsifal* is Christian or pagan can also be put in the way Kierkegaard would have done. Truth is subjective, only the truth that edifies is truth for you. Parsifal cannot accept or even understand the truth of others, he receives truth in the moment of empathy. In this timeless moment he finds the truth that edifies him. The truth for him becomes Monsalvat, its community, the Grail and the redemption of the Redeemer. What does it mean to redeem the Redeemer? Whatever interpretation we choose they all arrive at the conclusion that Parsifal has found the truth.

As opposed to *Parsifal*, there is little essential controversy in the interpretations of *Tristan and Isolde* (1859). This music drama remains close to the Greek model with its Aristotelian unity of time, place, and action. It is also close to Lukács's dictum that tragic heroes are already dead when they first appear on stage. This drama is also Greek in that the past is related by the servant, Brangene, who replaces the female chorus. Everything is fated, not by the magic potion but by the past and by the protagonists themselves. Why then is this wonderful music drama not a tragedy? How can death through love, personal redemption in love as the highest ecstasy be tragic at all? I do not say that it is less than tragedy but that it is different.

Wagner worked on the *Ring* tetralogy throughout almost his whole productive life. As George Bernard Shaw said, he could not have finished it earlier because it is the drama of his time, of European history in the second half of the century. In the first version, written during the 1848/49 revolutions, Siegfried was supposed to conquer the world and capitalism, the world of merchants, bourgeois pettiness and bring about its downfall. Even in the final version the obsession with gold and the hunger for wealth remain the source of all evils. The whole world, the modern world perishes, the downfall of our gods buries everyone and everything under the ruins of Valhalla. What remains is the other of history: nature, the Rhine. Even those who prefer the first Feuerbachian to the final Schopenhauerian version must admit that the latter's view of history was truer than the first version – truer as artwork.

Even a Wagner lover cannot read the drama cycle in the originally planned way: especially not after World War Two. Not simply because of the Nazi adoration of Siegfried, but also because the contemporary eye sees the story in an entirely different way. This alternative reading not only corresponds to the *Ring* cycle as much as the traditional reading, it also corresponds to our own times.

Who is the hero of the *Ring* cycle if we look at with our eyes? Siegfried? Oh no! Siegfried is not just naïve, he is also stupid. He lets himself be governed by Wotan, he does everything according to Wotan's script. He is the actor who does not know that he is not the author of the role he plays. Is Siegfried a free man? Some Hegelians might say, perhaps he is a hero all the same, because he recognizes necessity. Yet, even those who accept the Hegelian conception, must admit that Siegfried does not recognizes why he is doing what he is doing. He knows neither Wotan's design nor that the old man, whose spear he breaks, is the leader of the gods. He does not even make a fatal mistake that would follow from his character, unless we accept that forgetting Brünnhilde is in his character. Siegfried is, indeed, only a naïve, ill-fated youth. Is it then a mistake that so many significant thinkers and artists acclaim the *Ring* cycle as Wagner's great masterpiece? Even as a tragedy? Not if we recognize that the real hero is Brünnhilde. If there is a free actor in this drama cycle it is Brünnhilde. She protects – against his father, Wotan's will – Siegmund, the free lover, from Hunding, the unloved, brutal husband of Sieglinde. She rescues Sieglinde from Wotan's rage so that she can give birth to her and Siegmund's son. Brünnhilde is free because she is disobedient and she will be punished for it. She gives up her immortality for mortal freedom. She is the one who commits a tragic mistake (worse than a mistake) as a result of the trick played on her by Hagen, the son of Alberich, the dwarf, whose stealing of the Rhine gold launches the whole story of Wagner's *Ring*. Brünnhilde discloses to Siegfried's enemies the only vulnerable spot on his body, a spot that she alone knows. She is also the one who chooses her death freely. If the *Twilight of the Gods* (1876) is a tragedy, then its hero is not Siegfried but Brünnhilde. Wagner surely did not want his work to be read in this way, but he completed this music drama just at the time dramatists, in search of tragic characters and free personalities, started to turn towards the 'second sex.'

Even though the term music drama was and remains associated with Wagner, another opera of the age could have been called music drama as well: Mussorgsky's *Boris Godunov* (1874). The drama of the two usurpers of the Russian Czar's throne was written by Pushkin at the time historical dramas became popular in the German-speaking states and in France. When I spoke about the new cult of national history I referred to philosophical parallels, such as the grand narrative and the discovery of dialectics. I do not see, however, any signs of these concerns in Pushkin's play. There is only one resemblance between Pushkin and Schiller: the concern for the historical roots of the present. They share, however, no common historical past. In Schiller men are still living and dying for their idea, or at least they have ideas worthy of living or dying for, whereas in Pushkin there is nothing but commands and slavery, fear and obedience, with the exception of a poor idiot, who speaks the truth and is capable of empathy and still has faith. What a contrast between Pushkin's idiot and Nietzsche's madman! Pushkin was a late contemporary of Schiller, Mussorgsky a contemporary of Wagner, and yet 150 years later the Russian world is still the same.

4   The Will to Tragedy and Naturalism

The 'will to tragedy' is a kind of 'will to power' that has to confess its impotence. It was not by chance that Nietzsche was the first to spell out the will to tragedy in his long essay: *Richard Wagner in Bayreuth* (1876). We live in hopeless times, we need grandeur – at least on the stage. We need an anti-Alexander, who re-ties the Gordian knot and makes us European Greeks again. Nietzsche greeted Wagner as the modern tragic poet, who reawakened the sense of the tragic and the desire for tragic grandeur even in the lowly soul of modern man. Yet his tragedies do not promise the kind of future Schiller once dreamed of. The tragic hero of the *Ring* for Nietzsche is Wotan. The cycle encompasses the tragedy of the past and the coming end of the world, it does not hail a new world within the womb of the present. Nietzsche's will to tragedy is a challenge to mediocre bourgeois culture, and it is by the same token not present in

Wagner's great oeuvre. The reasons for Nietzsche's later disappointment with Wagner were already detectable in his early apotheosis. Nietzsche wanted the impossible: the rebirth of Greek tragedy as tragedies about the future waiting to be born from the present.

When Wagner's music dramas appeared on the scene, the dramatist Hebbel (1813–1863) was trying to revitalize the German dramatic spirit. Like Wagner, he turned to ancient stories, to legends, for example to the biblical story of *Judith* (1840) and even the *Nibelungen* myth (1862). However, none of Hebbel's pseudo-tragedies inspired by legends and myths was crowned with artistic success. His treatment of the material was artificial, without any relation to philosophical ideas or to the social or political conflicts of his own age. The will to tragedy was too obvious to have an effect. That Hebbel was nevertheless a great dramatist became apparent when he was not motivated by the will to tragedy but turned to a less ambitious subject, writing a domestic family drama: *Maria Magdalena* (1844). Hebbel's play is a brilliant link between Lessing and Ibsen, between *Emilia Galotti* and *Hedda Gabler*. The story is simple, it is no longer about a girl becoming the victim of a prince in the conflict between feudal habits and burgher morality but about a girl becoming the victim of bourgeois, Victorian ethics. All the men around Clara, her father, her brother, her childhood lover, her worthless, money hungry fiancé, despite their mutual dislike represent the same prejudices. Even the childhood love, who appreciates her candid confession that she is not a virgin, says that no one could marry her after such a confession. Clara is ready to have her child in her unmarried state, but she cannot expose her father to mortal shame that would surely kill him. She chooses instead the mortal sin of suicide and killing her child to avoid the father's shame. The drama ends with the father's words: 'I do not understand the world anymore.'

The drama is not a tragedy since Clara does not fight against the prejudices of men, she does not even challenge them. She commits suicide like thousands of seduced girls, who lost their 'honour' at that time. Ibsen's Hedda Gabler will also commit suicide, not, however, as a victim of the world of men but as a rebel against the world of male mediocrity. Suicide is her personal embodiment of the will to tragedy. We have arrived at the threshold of a new world: the world of women's emancipation. Women's emancipation was not just a movement, it signalized a turning point in the whole history of *homo sapiens*. All the traditional gender roles became questionable, the old and the new collided once again as in the time of the classical tragedies.

In the second half of the 19th century the social role of women as presented in drama began to change. Relations between men and women became problematic for both sides. When I said that the real hero of the *Ring* is not Siegfried but Brünnhilde I did not mean that Wagner became a 'feminist' but that he felt the spirit of history. Dramatists now took sides. They could give voice to women suffering under and rebelling against male supremacy or they could give voice to male uneasiness, even hatred against women, who challenged their historic role and dominated them instead of accepting subordination. Ibsen will present the first, Strindberg the second standpoint. Not just in my understanding but also in theirs. Sexual desire and even sexual pathology became at the turn of century one of the main motives in the dramas of Strindberg and others. Strindberg inherited from Nietzsche the struggle with the experience of the 'death of God,' his main concern, however, was psychological, the struggle of sexes, his repulsion against female desire.

The will to tragedy was a reaction to 'decadence,' to impotence, to the loss of grandeur. It was a reaction to a peaceful and prosaic present, where nothing happened to live or to die for. This was one of the motivations in 1914 for the general enthusiasm, above all of intellectuals, for the Great War. One of the most representative examples of the will to tragedy in this period was *Salome* (1905) by Richard Strauss. He termed his work a music drama to emphasize his debt to Wagner. Strauss was also a lover of Nietzsche's philosophy and in *Also sprach Zarathustra* composed a musical companion to Nietzsche's *Zarathustra*. The text of *Salome* was written by Oscar Wilde, the author of successful comedies. In *Salome*, however, he tried, he said, to introduce the language of Shakespeare into modern drama. The outcome was entirely inadequate for a modern drama, the language sounded affected and unnatural, like that of other 'decadent' dramatists, including the mythological dramas of Hebbel. Nevertheless, Wilde's play was a brilliant libretto for a music drama. Morbid sexual tensions within the royal family and in Salome's desire for a chaste religious fanatic, John the Baptist, lead to the murder of both John and Salome. Their deaths are not tragic, that is, they are not the consequence of a rational or emotional decision or of a moral sin but of sexual pathology (we are in the time of Freud).

The last writer, who attempted to write a tragedy motivated by the will to tragedy, was Paul Ernst. I mention him only because his *Brunhild* (1909) inspired Lukács to write his philosophical essay *The Metaphysics of Tragedy*. Tragic are the times where gods have already left the world. Paul Ernst believed that after the death of God tragedy had again became possible. In his discussion of tragedy as a metaphysical genre Lukács comes to the opposite conclusion. History is unfitted for tragic presentation – as Ernst's other tragedies prove. Moreover, a democratic age is not tragic: realism contradicts tragedy. Thus, the tragedies of Hebbel and Ernst have ethical but not poetical significance. The truly ethical for Lukács calls for a merger of two ethics: the ethics of Nietzsche and the ethics of Kierkegaard. The strict division between high and low (high and low love in Ernst's *Brunhild*) is the ethical line of division for Nietzsche, whereas the effort to become oneself that characterizes all tragic heroes, who are already dead when they appear on the scene, echoes the 'existential choice' of Kierkegaard.

Kierkegaard was not only a lifelong inspiration for the great Norwegian dramatist Ibsen (1828–1906) but also the protagonist of one of his early dramas, *Brand* (1866). With this work Scandinavian drama appeared on the European stage. It was not a dramatic success since it was perhaps the most characteristic example of the will to tragedy. Written in verse in five acts (as tragedies are supposed to be written) the drama is full of philosophical monologues. The hero Brand was modelled on Kierkegaard, a Kierkegaard without humour or irony. In his monologues Brand repeats Kierkegaard's idea of the existential choice: you choose yourself, becoming yourself is the purpose of life, since if you are ever untrue to your choice you lose yourself. Either Or: everything or nothing, says Brand, who chooses himself as 'the knight of faith,' the 'real follower of Christ' against the so-called Christians of his age. Ibsen's model for the knight of faith is Kierkegaard's Abraham and his readiness to sacrifice his son Isaac. That Kierkegaard identified his father with Abraham is well known. However, he never considered himself or his father tragic characters. He even emphasized that the knight of faith is not tragic, for the teleological suspension of the ethical cannot be tragic. In a tragedy a hero sacrifices something for an ethical cause, not, however, in order to remain like Brand what he chooses to be (a knight of faith). Ibsen portrays a Kierkegaard who sacrifices his son and his wife for the sake of remaining a knight of faith, who never compromises between everything and nothing and therefore never chooses something. This is not tragic because there is no place for a tragic mistake, when passion and goal are both self-oriented. The will to tragedy comes to naught.

Ibsen drew consequences from *Brand*. In *Peer Gynt* (1867) the hero learns the difference between 'being yourself' and 'being sufficiently yourself.' In his later plays, at the time when enlightenment and personal identity had become problematic, Ibsen wrote the most significant examples of the bourgeois dramas of which Diderot dreamt. However, the Aristotelian model still applied: where someone commits a tragic mistake *catharsis* is still possible.

Some major drama writers of the age turned towards the prosaic world both for poetic and ethical inspiration. They put on the stage the hunger for wealth, position, even banal experiences like suffering from hunger or debt. They presented a world that had been hitherto the domain of comedy. We are presented with cases of prosaic grandeur in daily life, in the intimate or the civil sphere, not on the battlefield. This is a world where the oppressed and the repressed – frequently women – revolt. Since comedy and serious plays by now share the stage, it is not always possible to categorize them. This difficulty is not entirely new. Moliere's *Misanthrope* cannot be termed simply as a comedy. From the end of 19th century onwards this uncertainty becomes the rule not the exception.

In Hegelian dialectics A is followed by non-A, and so it was in drama around the turn of the century: against the will to tragedy the will to anti-tragedy appeared. Let me recall Aristotle's distinction between historiography on the one hand and philosophy and tragedy on the other hand. Whereas the first tries to describe how things and events happened, tragedy and philosophy present what might be and what might have happened. Or to turn to Hegel's distinction between reality and actuality: actuality is not just real but the unity between essence and appearance. Anti-tragedy is conceived both in theory and in practice as drama without a transcendental sphere or transcendental idea, drama in which speech is not stylized and which gets as close to reality, to historiography as possible. The stage has to show people as they really are, as they really speak and as they really act. This tendency was termed Naturalism. Perfect naturalism is impossible and that is why I speak as far as naturalistic drama is concerned about the will to anti-tragedy.

Naturalist writers are sincere. They do not pretend to dwell (like Nietzsche) on the mountain peaks, they feel safe on the dirty earth. They repeat Diderot's and Lessing's gambit of putting simple men on the stage instead of kings or queens. In Diderot and Lessing's time those 'simple men' were burghers and merchants. Characters that earlier peopled the comic stage now occupy the stage of tragic or serious plays. At the end of the 19th century, the pattern repeated itself. Instead of bourgeois figures, the exploited workers, the hungry, the homeless, vagrants, prostitutes and drunken peasants will play the leading roles in serious drama. Their story should be real and empirical. Since common people do not use the language of flowers, the text of the drama cannot be poetical. Monologues are excluded because inner thoughts cannot be experienced. No distinction between essence and appearance is permitted since this distinction does not apply to everyday language and life.

Different theoretical tendencies and historical experiences coincide in the works of anti-tragedy. Social philosophy separated from philosophy to become sociology. As opposed to philosophy, sociology is not supposed to dwell on the transcendental level. To speak with Kant: in sociology everything should be open to experience, for nothing in a proposition is scientific if the content cannot be experienced. Sociological theories thus became the servants of empirical verification. Max Weber was still sufficiently philosophically inspired to introduce 'ideal types' into his theory, even though his *Economy and Society* tried to remain on empirical ground. Just as sociology detached itself from social philosophy, so psychology separated itself from the philosophy of the spirit. Every nuance of the empirical psyche became as important as the grand passions. Although Freud's theory was essentially philosophical, his theory and method of psychoanalysis were largely understood empirically or quasi-empirically. The other radical philosophy running parallel with anti-tragic drama was Marxism, interpreted as a science or as an ideology, translated into empirical life mainly via the needs of the trade unions and social democratic movements.

I will exemplify naturalist drama, that is, anti-tragedies of social-Marxian inspiration, with the early plays of two well-known writers: Gerhart Hauptmann's *The Weavers* (1892) and Maxim Gorky's *The Lower Depths* (1902). Both plays were extremely influential. Both represent anti-tragedy as naturalism, putting an end to poetic language.

The characters of Hauptmann's play are weavers and their families at the time of their revolt in the 1840s, the first rebellion of German workers. The author knew the story already as a child since it was told him by his grandfather. The weavers and their families are suffering – not from love, not even from lack of political liberty, not even from sexual desire or prejudice and there is nothing refined or elevated about their suffering. They suffer from hunger, they are unable to feed their children. The wages they receive for their hard work are not enough even for buying bread or for burying their dead. The capitalist owner of the factory is a heartless man, who despises the workers. If he decided to pay higher wages he would soon be bankrupt because his employees will drink even more. These are sentences everyone had already heard a thousand times (at least in my childhood) before going to the theatre. Now, however, the scenes of the starving weavers and their longing for bread remind one of a concentration camp without barbed wire.

We immediately notice the common feature of all naturalist plays. They do not begin with dialogue but with a detailed description of the room, the furniture and all the persons present, together with their activities, in addition also the exact time of the events. We first see a room in the capitalist Dreissiger's house. It is mid day, a hot May day and the workers are waiting in line for their pay. They are cheated of what is due to them with various tricks. One person stands out from the crowd, Backer, with his stubbornness. He alone is defending his right. We immediately sense that he will be the leader of the revolt. The play shows how the weavers turn from passivity to activity, finally to violence against their unfeeling exploiters. The army arrives, the shooting starts, corpses are left on the scene. Then the unexpected happens, the weavers drive the military from the village. Hurrah! The spectator feels the spirit of mass movement and understands the choreography of a new kind of mass action. How and why did it start, how will it develop and what kind of a person will emerge out of the mass and take over leadership? The characters of the various weavers are just sketches and they are just types. The story moves with the movement of the crowd. Irrespective of individual character, the weavers become a crowd because they share the same grievances. Hauptmann was of course not the first to present the movement of a crowd in the history of drama. Shakespeare already had in *Julius Caesar* and other tragedies. Hauptmann, however, was engaged in something new, something different: the crowd of the *Weavers* is not incited by a demagogue, its movement is entirely spontaneous. This is why I speak of choreography and this is why the title is not the name of a single protagonist. In this play all together form the one protagonist, the collective as collective subject.

In Gorky's second drama *The Lower Depths* the protagonist is the setting, the shelter described at the beginning of every act in great detail, a rundown space rented by a variety of homeless people. Unlike *The Weavers* nothing extraordinary happens. What changes is the space and as a result the social place of the characters. The inhabitants of the asylum are all lost people, lost to the world and to themselves, or as they put it, they have become 'superfluous people.' Once they were somebody, a baron or an actor, now they are nobodies, who have lost not just what they had but themselves as well. The stories we learn from these superfluous people are stories that happen everywhere. Small stories, mostly banal and average. For example: jealousy between sisters, violence resulting from it, but without *catharsis* or any kind of solution. A woman dies of tuberculosis – a favourite topics of novels, short stories, plays and operas from *La dame aux camélias* by Dumas the younger to *La Traviata*. A young alcoholic tries in vain to get rid of his addiction. What also makes this a naturalist play is that there is no 'drama' in this drama. Almost no one notices when the woman dies, least of all her husband and no one is interested in the past glory of the alcoholic actor. The jealousy between the sisters – the older sister beats the younger almost to death – attracts interest only for a short time. The inhabitants of the asylum are closed in themselves; their thoughts or daydreams centre on their own selves and not on others – as is generally the case in life.

Still, these characters are and remain individuals. The poet creates a miracle: the audience do not perceive the superfluous people as superfluous. Gorky achieves this miracle by introducing a very Russian character, who comes from the outside and leaves again at the end. He is Luka, the wanderer, the 'good man.' The good man discovers common humanity and personal possibility in every 'superfluous' man and woman. In his eyes no one is superfluous. The impact of Dostoevsky on the whole of Russian literature is evident. The good man recognizes the potential in all the inhabitants of the asylum, encourages them to live up to their possibilities and makes them believe that they can: all in vain.

Naturalist drama claims to tell the truth about human life. It looks like an internal contradiction that these dramas are socially, politically, and ideologically motivated. From the 1860s up to the First World War they make statements about the conflicts of their times – the 'social question' and the 'gender question.' In *The Weavers* and *The Lower Depths* the social question occupies the central position. Gorky was already a committed socialist before the Russian revolution of 1905, and although the young Hauptmann was not a socialist, his play was regarded by the leading critic of the German Social-Democratic Party, Franz Mehring, as their play.

Strindberg (1849–1912) also addresses the 'social question' in his dramas, but his main interest and passion is vested in the 'gender question.' He is strongly ideologically partisan, as in his polemics against Ibsen. Strindberg calls his plays tragedies even though they are not. In the introduction to *Miss Julie* (1888) he says that where a family tradition is dying there is tragedy. This is the case in his drama *The Father* (1887), a drama highly praised by Nietzsche. In the preface to *Miss Julie*, Strindberg shares with the readers his judgment on society, drama and literature in general. This judgment serves as a guideline for the understanding of his work. He criticizes 'the middle-class immobility' of the soul in Dickens' novels and praises Naturalism for introducing into literature the fluctuating, changing human psyche. What interests the audience is not the logical but the psychological process. They want to know the mechanism not just the machine. This has been best achieved, he contends, in the documentary novels of the Goncourt brothers.

Strindberg's dramas, above all *The Father* and *Miss Julie,* were perceived in their time as outspoken or disgusting for presenting sexual desire openly, that is, naturalistically. In *Miss Julie* there is a scandalous sexual relation between the countess and her valet. The topic soon became popular because it was hailed as talking finally about sex openly in high culture, in literature. What is most important in Strindberg is that a sexual game is not presented by him as sexual game but as a power game. Sexual relations are power relations. Strindberg hates women and is afraid of women, because he believes that the conflict will end with the victory of women. In *The Father* – it is not by chance that the father is a captain – the conflict begins over the education of the daughter. Who decides about a daughter's education, the father or the mother? Who dominates whom? The power struggle leaves the man weak and he becomes obsessed by doubt whether he is really the father of his child. Only the mother can really know, men can never know. The psychodrama unfolds with the wife turning into a demonic dominatrix. The fallen father is neither murdered nor does he commit suicide, he simply dies of a stroke.

In *Miss Julie* the gender question is mixed with the social question. Jean, the valet, is on many counts superior to Miss Julie (he is, after all, a man). For Miss Julie, it is a shame and a humiliation to fall in love with and make love to a valet. The social weapon is used by both parties. He says a man can make a woman a countess but a woman cannot make a man a count. When she says, I am the daughter of a count, he replies, I can become father of a count. In the development of the play the social and the psychological merge more and more. Miss Julie is revealed as an 'unnatural' woman because her mother was a feminist who lived with the friend of her father. In turn, Julie, who loves and hates her father, swore to her mother that she will never become the slave of a man. This drama, like *The Father, The Weavers* or *Lower Depths,* ends without an end. This is the anti-tragic end, things always repeat themselves, there is no *catharsis.*

5 Ibsen and Chekhov

It is said that just before you die of tuberculosis you feel healthy again and very much alive. This is what happened with 'classic' drama. At the end of the 19th and the beginning of the 20th century Europe was blessed again with two great geniuses of the theatre: Ibsen and Chekhov. Diderot, Lessing and Schiller dreamt of the project of a new tragedy with common people as heroes, yet without success. Their dramas lacked the tragic spirit. The everyday life of domestic figures was somehow unfitted, not because they did not suffer or were less ambitious or even less cruel but because the stakes were private. Thus, in Ibsen's *John Gabriel Borkman* (1896) the hero is possessed by the will to power and compares himself to Napoleon. But what is at stake? His position as the director of a bank and his plans for a huge investment. And what is his sin? Embezzling his clients' money, or borrowing his investors' money, as he preferred to call it. Does this make Borkman a Napoleon? Even if he were successful (despite his crime) and could have satisfied his hunger for power, he could never become a Napoleon, only a Rockefeller or a Morgan.

Had Ibsen shared the will to tragedy he would have satisfied it in his early historical drama about Julian the Apostate, *The Emperor and the Galilean* (!873). There was no follow up, however. It was not Ibsen who entertained the will to tragedy but some of his heroes and heroines – at least, if not the will to tragedy, the wish for tragedy and desire for grandeur. Ibsen took the opposite path to

Schiller and Hebbel, he proceeded not from bourgeois drama towards historical drama but the other way around. The real Ibsen is the Ibsen of bourgeois drama. However, the inspiration of Kierkegaard that we encountered in *Brand* remained strong in his later prosaic dramas. The question: how to become who we are, how to remain true to ourselves, and its reverse: how do we lose ourselves, become living corpses, these questions remain in the centre of all Ibsen's dramas. They are existential dramas about life as it appears or develops in a world of pettiness. This theme, very much in the spirit of Kierkegaard's judgment of his times, makes Ibsen's dramas complex. God is no longer a spectator, as he still was in Shakespeare's or in Racine's time. In Ibsen God is dead. Christianity has ceased to be a form of life, it has become either a habit or the conservative politics of moral prejudice, one of Ibsen's (and Nietzsche's) main 'spectres.'

There are two hierarchies in Shakespeare: a hierarchy of grandeur and a hierarchy of virtue (Hamlet/Horatio). There is neither grandeur nor virtue in Ibsen's dramas: grandeur and virtue are not only relative in comparison to other virtues, they are also vacillating, that is, dependent on the audience or readers, on the historical times and places, finally on the performance. In *A Doll's House* (1879) and *An Enemy of the People* (1882), however, Ibsen's judgment or rather sympathy is unambivalent. Here dissatisfied spectators or readers have to fight the author's judgment not that of the characters. This is not the case in his other dramas. Take *Rosmersholm* ((1886). Johannes Rosmer is certainly a man considered 'decadent' in Ibsen's time; earlier he would have been considered a melancholic, nowadays perhaps depressive. Is he a virtuous man, sincere, deeply humane as Rebecca sees him or a sublime egoist? Is Relling's principle in *The Wild Duck* ((1884) that if one robs a philistine of the lie of his life one also robs him of his happiness right or wrong? More precisely: is it more virtuous to let people lie to themselves or to enlighten them that their lives are founded on lies? Is Werle Greger in *A Doll's House*, who attacks everyone with his ideals just a ridiculous clown or a dangerous agitator? Is it always bad if you attack others with ideal claims? In *Pillars of Society* (1877) it is virtuous rather than bad. In Ibsen's dramas all the theses, ideas and actions of the characters are contextual, their value in the hierarchy of virtues or vices changes according to the person who advances them, the situation and the persons addressed. However, in *The Wild Duck* an innocent child is the victim – and that settles the judgment.

Ibsen's heroes are just ordinary people. However, in the soul of these common people, especially artists, the desire to be great and even tragic has taken root. Ibsen portrayed this desire symbolically. The ambition to rise is symbolized by climbing, as in climbing to the top of a mountain – Rubek in *When*

We Dead Awaken (1899) – or climbing to the top of the tower – Solness in *The Master Builder* (1892). Both Rubek and Solness are artists – the first a sculptor, the second a master builder – who once created great works and became famous but have lost the capacity to match their earlier achievement. The problematic of these two dramas became central later with the question whether artists should sacrifice life for art, just as the conflict between business interests and ecology, raised in *An Enemy of the People,* is much more actual today than in Ibsen's time.

Rubek and Solness try to reach the heights again to live up to the high expectations of a woman. With the exception of Stockmann, the doctor in *An Enemy of the People,* who alone fights for truth and life, Ibsen's women are stronger than the men. Ibsen is not Strindberg, however. Both experience something similar but they feel and judge differently. Strindberg hates women, Ibsen is interested in them and even pays tribute to them. In some of his dramas women are more nearly tragic characters than the men. Not all his men are weak. Helmer in *A Doll's House* is an egoistic, self–indulgent philistine who keeps his wife Nora as a plaything. Nora is the only one of Ibsen's main female characters who rebels and becomes free in life not in death by discovering that she has been living with strangers. Her father and her husband are these strangers. She leaves her family to find and become herself. But her task is, so to speak, easy in Ibsen's terms since her husband is not afraid of the voice of conscience, only of the regard of others, of shame (what will people say, what will happen to me). It's worth noting that Ibsen portrays here the situation that became central in 20th century existentialism, in Sartre and particularly in Simone de Beauvoir's *Second Sex.* According to Beauvoir, it is the regard of men that creates women. Women try to live up to men's regard and to act in the way men expect them to act and to behave. How can a woman liberate herself? Only by reversing this regard, by looking at men with women's eyes. This is how *A Doll's House* ends. Nora looks at Helmer with her own eyes and sees another man: an egoistic coward, who does not even know what loving means. And then, Helmer also begins to see himself as he was created by Nora's regard.

Why are most men in Ibsen's dramas weak? I am sure that Ibsen did not know the work of the young Kant on the beautiful and the sublime, nevertheless, some of his women are modelled in the spirit of young Kant. The conscience of men is not robust, says Hilda in *The Master Builder.* What did Kant say? That men have to control their emotions by morality, and this makes them melancholy, whereas if they fail to control their emotions they remain simple egoists. Women, on the contrary, do the right thing so to speak by instinct. Rosmer in *Rosmersholm* and Solness in *The Master Builder* both suffer from the feeling of guilt for what they wish and desire. (Remember Racine's Phaedra, who sinned only in desire. She had a fragile conscience unlike Theseus.) Solness does not cause the fire but he desires it and profits from it, Rosmer does not cause his wife's suicide but secretly wishes for it, since he is in love with Rebecca, and his wife feels herself superfluous. Hilda is right, Solness's conscience is not robust, this is why he is dizzy on the top of the steeple. And Rebecca tries in vain to transform Rosmer into a happy social reformer, but the opposite happens. Rosmer is not a fighter and Rebecca loses her taste for a happy life.

After leaving behind the traditional type of the eternally faithful women, a Solveig, there are two main types of modern women in Ibsen. The rebel, the emancipated women, like Nora, and the women who want to be great and famous by finding a great man, a genius and helping him to become famous and thus shining in the light of his brilliance, like a Lou Salome or an Alma Mahler. Ibsen's heroines of the second type are not so lucky, their men are not geniuses like Nietzsche, Freud or Mahler, just weak men without any talent. They dream about the future fame of their men, but these men are not even great in their death. Ibsen's most outstanding woman character of this type, the heroine of *Hedda Gabler* (1890), is the wife of a young, terribly boring but goodhearted bookworm, who invests her hopes in a childhood friend, the author of a supposedly wonderful book, imagining him crowned with glory or as a hero who commits suicide. Her hero, however, is an alcoholic, who dies in the salon of an elegant whore by accident. Hedda Gabler loses her bet, her goal. Exposed to blackmail and solitude, she is the one who commits suicide, she is the 'man.' The clashes between the sexes, between generations, between conservative and liberal ideas, between patricians and plebeians overlap and interact in all of Ibsen's plays.

It has often been pointed out that Ibsen follows the model of classical Athenian tragedy. The past always returns to pass judgment on the living. There is no chorus, the past returns in personal narratives or in dialogues between people who meet again, perhaps after a long time, and recover their common past. The curse returns in these dialogues, the ghosts of the past appear. There are inherited biological ghosts like syphilis, in which the vice of the fathers takes revenge on the sons. Ghosts can also be social, as in the inherited judgments of the fathers which become fatal prejudices for the sons and daughters, just as lethal as syphilis. Finally, ghosts can be personal in for example the inherited incapability to love that kills love in the soul of others.

Chekhov (1860–1904), the other great genius of the turn of century was not just a dramatist. His short stories are classics of the genre between Maupassant and Thomas Mann. I will speak only about the spirit or philosophy of his dramatic works, starting with *The Seagull* (1896) and concentrating on *The Three Sisters* (1900) and *The Cherry Orchard* (1903). In Chekhov's time Russia was utterly politicized. The leading theorists were literary and cultural critics with a strong political agenda such as Chernyshevsky or Dobroljubov. Chekhov is the exception. No politics but much philosophy – for those who notice it, especially in *The Three Sisters* and *The Cherry Orchard*.

Hegel remarked that everything happens in the world twice: first as tragedy and then as comedy. For Kierkegaard, tragedies themselves may become comedies when the age itself becomes comic. As we saw, several scenes or figures in Ibsen are comic, or at least they can be played as if they were comic. Chekhov went further when he called some of his dramas farces and suggested that they should be played as farces. Indeed, all his dramas can be read and played in two ways: to reduce the audience to tears or to make the audience burst out laughing. The word tragicomedy might be misleading, for Chekhov avoided *catharsis* on purpose, as did Brecht later.

It still makes sense, however, to call Chekhov dramas tragicomic since most of them concern people who could have been heroes of tragedies earlier: they are nobles rather than bourgeois, former great landowners, generals and the flower of the nation. They have become comic, not because they lost their wealth, land, castles and political positions, but because they became petty. A general, a landowner is even more ridiculous than a bourgeois in the same situation, not personally but because his ancestors were members of the imperial court, even former boyars, who could have been leading characters of tragedies. A comic world populated by formerly noble characters becomes an absurd world: tragicomedy transmuted into absurd drama.

Before I examine the philosophical message in Chekhov's dramas, I need to mention the philosophical aspect of their composition, especially in the case of *The Three Sisters* and *The Cherry Orchard*. When they were first played, the audience was utterly dissatisfied, even shocked. Nothing happens! All the three acts are alike! What kind of drama is this? From Schiller through to Wagner and Ibsen audiences can be satisfied or dissatisfied with the plot because there is a plot. Some of Ibsen's plays are almost 'thrillers.' But where is the plot in *The Three Sisters* and *The Cherry Orchard*? Or in *Uncle Vanya* (1896) and *The Seagull*, where the end returns to the beginning? In between something happened but by the end it is as if nothing has happened. From *The Seagull* onwards Chekhov's plays are not only anti-tragedies, they are also anti-dramas.

Staging a play is always a hermeneutic exercise. *Antigone* or *Hamlet* or *Emilia Galotti* cannot be put on stage as comedies. There are often comic characters in modern tragedies and serious dramas but the plot leads us away from understanding serious plays as comedy, not only because someone dies but because of the way they die. Modern hermeneutics influenced and keeps influencing theatre. Productions more and more depend on interpretation. Should a drama be played as tragedy or a comedy? Chekhov probably did not know Schleiermacher's conception of hermeneutics, but he did know Nietzsche, who together with Kierkegaard was the first hermeneutic philosopher. With Gadamer, we can say that Chekhov is looking at the tradition with a very contemporary eye. Chekhov knew what Ibsen only guessed, that his plays can have at least two entirely different readings and that it depends on the director and the audience. In *The Seagull* young Constantine commits suicide, However, he can still be played as a comic figure quite authentically, not to speak of Tusenbach's death in a stupid duel in *The Three Sisters*.

Chekhov had two main lines of succession: George Bernard Shaw on the one hand, the absurd comedy of Beckett and Ionesco on the other. The main objection against Chekhov dramas in his time was the absence of plot. Everything remains the same and everything gets repeated! Doesn't this describe Beckett's *Waiting for Godot*? And what about the genre? Ionesco term his *Chairs* 'tragic farce,' *The Lesson* 'a comic drama,' *The Bald Soprano* an 'anti-play.' My reference to *Godot* was not meant to point out an interesting coincidence but something essential. The essence of non-happenings in *The Three Sisters* and in *The Cherry Orchard* is that all of the characters are waiting for Godot.

Drama always takes place in the present and historical drama is no exception. The past is within the present from Sophocles to Ibsen. The protagonists are not just inheriting an estate or even a kingship, they also inherit with them merits and sins, they carry the glory or the fate of their families and must answer for their own deeds. In Chekhov there is no present or rather there is nothing but the present. Time stands still. This is why there is no plot. The past exists not as a ghost but as the object of nostalgia in place or in time or both: Moscow and life in Moscow in *The Three Sisters,* the wonderful cherry orchard from the time before the emancipation of serfs. It is obvious from the beginning of *The Three Sisters* that they will never return to Moscow, just as it is obvious that the great cherry orchard is full of dying trees, which no longer bear fruit and no longer produce a profit – only debts.

The Three Sisters and *The Cherry Orchard* are tragicomedies of utopian thinking. In these plays utopia is either behind us (Moscow or the cherry orchard) or before us (the wonderful future life after we are dead). The gap between the present reality and the dream world could not be greater. The portrayal of these utopias is not satirical but deeply ironical because we both laugh at the characters and pity them, sometimes even love one of them. The first kind of utopia is not utopian as such, for to begin a new life, to give up drinking or playing cards, to stop wasting money, to start working, to study and to marry are all fairly rational goals. They become utopian in the context in which they are formulated. They remain daydreams, since work is boring for Irina and to marry is boring for Masha in *The Three Sisters*, because life itself is boring. The second type of utopia is traditional: the personal afterlife. We keep on living and God will reward us in the afterlife, as Sonia says at the end of *Uncle Vanya*.

The third kind of utopia is the most interesting because it is ironical and sometimes satirical, not only for the author but several times also for those who voice it. It is a model that can be summed up like this: 'we are suffering here, we are bored, yet three or four hundred years from now, our suffering and pain will be crowned by success. There will be a wonderful world. There will be justice and wellbeing and people will live happily.' This utopia appears in two variations. These happy people will not remember us, although we prepared the way for them, or second, these happy people will remember us as the ones who worked and suffered for them. Both versions are ironical, not just because the characters who voice them do not make any contribution to this brilliant future but also because Chekhov is more than sceptical about the idea of progress, as it was generally believed and expressed by the intelligentsia in Russia and elsewhere at the end of the 19th century. Chekhov's characters are waiting for this brilliant future and talking about it just like Vladimir and Estragon talking about Godot, who will certainly come. When he will come is not really important for Chekhov's characters any more than for Vladimir and Estragon. They will be never disappointed because daydreams can only disappoint if they come true.

Chekhov understands and even loves some of his characters. He shares their pains and hopes while he is laughing. One needs to hope in something if life cheats one out of everything, even if it is one's own fault. Checkov's Russia is rural Russia, the Russia of a bankrupt aristocracy and loyal servants, of a military without tasks, of an intelligentsia of artists and the educated. There are no heroes and heroines, just bankrupt characters, bankrupt ways of life as presented and represented by a few very different characters. These anti-dramas of the twilight of the gods, of the Russian landed aristocracy and of the remnants of old Russia have nothing to do with Naturalism, even if they served as a kind of model for Gorki in *The Lower Depths*.

There are different kinds of irony. In *The Three Sisters* and especially in *The Cherry Orchard* Chekhov portrays some losers with great empathy. Ljubov Andrievna for example is a noble even if entirely irrational soul or perhaps it is because of her irrationality that she is a noble soul. Nobility is a kind of moral beauty. The main victim of this anti-drama drama is not she, however, but the cherry orchard, the trees and the beauty of the landscape. Beauty becomes useless and old. The old servant, the son of a serf who is left behind at the end of the play, shares the fate of the orchard. Chekhov mourns beauty. This is his unique feature in comparison to other dramatists: nowhere else have

I encountered the mute suffering of nature as the protagonist of a drama. Every Chekhov play is named after the main character except for the one mute heroine: the dying beauty of the cherry orchard.

The metamorphosis of drama of which I have been speaking started in a few dramas by Ibsen to become obvious in Chekhov's 'tragicomic' plays. The audience did not know whether they were supposed to cry or to laugh. In my plays everything is about love, said Chekhov, but what kind of love. George Bernard Shaw (1856–1950) drew the consequences. His plays with one exception are comedies in all the different subgenres of comedy. One could object that *Saint Joan* (1923) is not comic. It is, however, highly ironical and sometimes satirical. It is a play written in Kierkegaard's spirit because there is not a single Christian in this Christian play, with the exception of Joan herself, who is burned at the stake. Her execution is motivated by sheer politics. The English dignitaries as well as the inquisitor speak in the play like English lords and clergymen spoke in Shaw's time. This is typical of all Shaw's 'historical plays.' His *Caesar and Cleopatra* (1898) was meant as an answer to Shakespeare. The great hero of the Roman history and the great heroine of love and intrigue are now actors on the comic stage. Caesar is like an aging British colonizer and Cleopatra like an Indian princess in Delhi. Shaw works with satire and irony, not with parody, however, even when he rewrites well-known stories. Taking a different perspective is not identical with parody. As we learn from the dream intermezzo in *Man and Superman* (1902) the difference between Heaven and Hell depends on the perspective. One can freely choose between going to Heaven or Hell. Moreover, Hell is a very pleasant place, since it is amusing, and one can speak freely about everything.

Shaw is a highly self-conscious writer. He knows Strindberg, Ibsen and Chekhov, he writes a book on Wagner, whom he adores. While shaping his characters he relies on all the radical philosophers and their followers or pretended followers. He consciously deconstructed the tragic stage. As he says in the 'philosophical' intermezzo of *Man and Superman,* everything depends on your perspective. Perspectives and personalities can be reversed. There are several comic 'conversions' in Shaw. I am thinking not only of *Captain Brassbound's Conversion* (1899) but also of the lovely play *The Devil's Disciple* (1896), where at the moment of trial the devil's disciple, that is, the anarchist, acts like a minister ready to become a martyr, whereas the minister acts like a soldier and anarchist. The reversal of personality is a traditionally tragic scene of catharsis. The reversals in Shaw are everything but cathartic. The only one of his plays Shaw calls a 'tragedy' is *The Doctor's Dilemma* (1906). This is an artist's drama, like *The Master Builder* by Ibsen, but in a more radical manner. Louis Dubedat is great painter and a great scoundrel. When confronted with his misdeeds, he makes a dying confession in an existentialist spirit and in the spirit of Nietzsche and Wagner. He is a painter and he chose himself as a painter and he never became untrue to himself, to the art of painting, he never lied in painting. He believes in Michelangelo, in Velasquez and in Rembrandt, that is, 'in the redemption of all things by Beauty everlasting, and the message of art that had made these hands blessed.' This is his religion.

I mentioned that Shaw re-visited all the topics of his predecessors or contemporaries: the so-called woman's question, as he calls it, modern marriage, generational conflict. He unmasks the opinions and theses of his characters as prejudices, but comic because these prejudices do not harm anyone who does not deserve it. Vivie Warren in *Mrs Warren's Profession* (1893) leaves her mother, just as Nora left her husband. She leaves her mother for good, not because she finds out that she earned her money, including for her own education, as a prostitute, but because the mother is ashamed and presents herself as a respectable bourgeois lady, that is, because her life is inauthentic. The war of sexes and the women's question is central in many of Shaw's works because it is also a 'man's question.' Like Strindberg or Ibsen, Shaw presents males as the weak gender. His women are more forceful and more rational, whether their rationality is moral or immoral. Everyone knows at least *Pygmalion* (1912) from its simplified musical version (*My Fair Lady*).

Man and Superman focuses on several of Shaw's fundamental themes and beliefs. The play is termed *A Comedy and a Philosophy* suggesting that the story itself is a comedy, whereas the inserted dream is philosophy. To my mind both are both. The story is an interpretation of the Don Juan story as Mozart presented it in *Don Giovanni*. Sometimes Shaw attaches to his text Mozart's score. Shaw's characters are of course modern and very British. John Tanner is Don Juan, Anne is Donna Anna, Octavius is Ottavio and so on. Anne's late father, in the form of the Statue, appears only in the dream section. The gender roles are reversed as in Ibsen's and Strindberg's plays. The woman gets what she wants and the weak man finally gives up. Anne chases Jack with lies and tricks from which he tries to escape in vain. Octavius loves Anne and wants to marry her, but she knows that Octavius will make a terrible husband while the author of the revolutionary handbook will make a good husband since he will not be boring and won't adore his wife as a goddess, but take her as she is – a manipulative liar. Shaw makes marrying Anne as much a punishment for John as being killed by the statue is for Don Juan. Shaw makes fun of reciprocated love not just in this play but also in several others (*Widower's Houses*, 1892). The romantic love of Octavius is unselfish and 'pure,' precisely because it is never reciprocated and never even really wants to be reciprocated.

In the dream of John Tanner heroes and heroines of Mozart enter into theoretical (philosophical) discussion with each other. In this discussion Schopenhauer, Freud, Nietzsche and Darwin are fused ironically: sex is motivated by the Life Force and by a kind of vital energy. The aim of the Life Force is to create the Superman (meant ironically). We laugh at the unmasking of prejudices and also authentic feelings and desires as prejudices. When Don Juan in the dream remarks that intellect has become unpopular in our days we cannot help laughing. Nothing is sadder than a good joke.

6 Sartre and Brecht

Radical philosophies exerted a far greater influence on drama than any other modern philosophy since Descartes. The ideas of radical philosophies were directly voiced in Wagner, Strindberg, Ibsen, Chekhov and Shaw. Why did radical philosophy alone exert such an essential influence on modern drama? One can point to other possible parallels such as that between the phenomenology of Husserl and Naturalism but the connection is indirect. There is also hermeneutics, for example Eugene O'Neill's *Mourning becomes Electra* (1931) is a modern interpretation of Greek myth or Shaw's reinterpretation of a historical legend in *Caesar and Cleopatra*. One could also say that Wagner's music dramas represent strong interpretations of medieval legends. The problem with this parallel is that the reinterpretation of myths and legends is as old as drama and opera in general. Monteverdi and Rameau reinterpret as does Shakespeare. Drama and opera was always political in the sense that major composers and writers refer to their own times and sometimes provide lessons to their times. It cannot be denied, however, that in the 20th century dramatists returned consciously to the old models, that is, that the hermeneutic project became conscious.

So, I ask again, why in the parallel story between philosophy and drama was it that the four radical philosophers of the 19th century became the main conspirators, in whose works dramatists discovered their own agenda? There are at least two connected reasons for the overwhelming influence of radical philosophy. As we have already seen, several branches of philosophy split away from philosophy in the post-Hegelian spiritual world. After Hegel (and sometimes earlier) natural sciences and social sciences emancipated themselves from philosophy. The belief that to be scientific means to be tested, true and unquestionable was widespread. Marx and Freud were certain that their project was through and through scientific and that their discoveries were tested and true. Kierkegaard considered himself a religious thinker. For him philosophy was identical with Hegel. Only Nietzsche was aware of practicing philosophy. Sociology, economics, psychology and even historiography regarded themselves as products of empirical research and open to empirical verification or, to quote Kant, as territories of possible experience. Even logic, one of the oldest philosophical topics, emancipated itself from philosophy, first as mathematical logic and then as analytical philosophy, the method of problem solving through demonstration and argumentation. Neo-Kantians divided the sciences: social sciences were supposed to operate not with explanation but interpretation, understanding. However, one cannot aspire to understanding human life or actions without referring to some transcendental ideas. A merely empirical social science cannot raise claims to Truth but only to the truth of facts.

There are at least two phenomena that cannot be entirely understood on empirical grounds. The phenomenon of religion (faith, belief and transcendence) and the phenomenon of the soul (psyche, desires, feeling and thinking) can only be understood through critique because critique cannot be practiced on merely empirical grounds. The critique of something has to be undertaken from a standpoint separate from the object of the critique, that is, imputed, transcendental and not empirical. Kant's critical system was based on this discovery. Philosophy, he said, is thinking in concepts (ideas) or reason. Hence philosophy's first task is self-understanding: showing the limits of the authority of pure reason itself. Radical philosophy preserved this distinction: the object, the target of the critic is empirical, and the weapon of the critic is transcendental. However, radical thinkers failed to recognize this when they claimed to be scientists. Marx claimed the factual validity of his transcendental idea of surplus value. For him the difference between empirical and transcendental depends on the position the scientist takes: if you take the position of the proletariat, your transcendental idea functions empirically.

I refer to Marxism, Freudianism, Existentialism, as philosophies, even if their founding fathers claimed to practice science or – as Kierkegaard once claimed – poetry. Their philosophies were interpreted and reinterpreted as 'isms', that is, from perspectives and positions historically dependent on time, place, political convictions and personal philosophical agendas. The different 'isms' were also frequently combined. Nietzsche and Freud, Marx and Freud are the most modern frequent combinations. Moreover, the three dominant philosophical schools after Hegel: phenomenology, philosophy of language and hermeneutics were also infected by radical philosophy, and vice versa. Heidegger was inspired by Husserl and Kierkegaard, Sartre by Husserl, Heidegger, Marx and Freud, Foucault by hermeneutics and all the radical philosophers. None of them will create their own 'isms,' even if they become fashionable for a time like Sartre. There were many schools after Hegel, but all significant philosophers will become individual thinkers (I come back to this question in the last section of this book). No wonder that the influence of radical philosophy lasted up the end of the 20th century and the end of European drama – 'the end of art.' Moreover, writers' commitment to radical philosophy became even more direct after 1900. I will concentrate on authors who were themselves philosophers or art theorists and expressed their conceptions both in their dramas and their theoretical writings: Sartre, the existentialist and Brecht, the Marxist saw it as their duty to influence their audience with their moral and political messages.

In the dramas of his first creative period, Sartre (1905–1980) wanted to make a case for his own existentialist philosophy and its central idea that humans are thrown into freedom. Every situation offers a possibility for free choice. He rhetorically emphasized this point in *The Flies (1943)* and *Morts sans Sépulture* (The Victors, 1946), which re-think and re-present traditional dramatic situations and conflicts. *The Flies* is a variation on the *Oresteia*, the second play depicts the conflicts of resistance fighters suffering from torture, loneliness and fear of being forgotten as they await execution (a typical scene in modern operas such as *Aida* or *Tosca*). The main question for Sartre is also traditional: are these dead on furlough strong enough not to confess under torture. The setting resembles Gorky's *Lower Depths*. Several persons are thrown into a confined space, they are all different but in the same situation. There is no central hero. There is even another similarity: one person comes from outside and leaves at the end: the leader of the resistance group Jean. They are all tortured in order to discover who this man is. Before they knew, they could not tell. Now that they know, they must remain silent. There is one young boy who cannot resist torture. His friends kill him, becoming murderers themselves (as Emilia Galotti is killed by her father to save her honour in Lessing's play). This is the moral conflict they face: they can act freely, despite not being free, because even under final duress one has a choice. Finally, all of them tell the truth when they know or at least believe that Jean is already safe – and will be executed all the same. This existentialist drama is very Kantian – one cannot foresee the consequences of one's action, but one knows the categorical imperative. The prisoners renounce the categorical imperative when they kill the boy for the sake of defending the leader, however, the consequences remain the same for them as not killing the boy: they are all executed. The moral lesson is the purpose of this directly political and historically concrete drama.

As a radical Brecht (1898-1956) was influenced by Marxism and applied it to the theatre in his own way. He made a case for what he called 'epic drama,' that is, a kind of drama that is not bound by unities of time and place but ranges across a longer period and in which the scenes concentrate on important and decisive conflicts at different times (several of Shakespeare's history plays are 'epic dramas'). Brecht rejected the Aristotelian theory of *catharsis*, and cathartic experience as well, since in his view they obstruct the political and moral learning process of the spectators. Empathy with the suffering characters that leads to the purification of our soul from self-pity and fear prevents the spectator from thinking about the lessons of the drama. One has to 'estrange' the plot and the characters in order to enable the audience to grasp the political and moral message and draw practical consequences from it. (Nothing is new under the philosophical sun. Who does not recognize Plato here?)

Among Brecht's works there are two plays that are to my mind the best historical dramas after Schiller: *The Life of Galileo* (1938) and *Mother Courage and Her Children* (1939). Both carry a political and moral message, but without Schiller's rhetoric, since it is the plot and not one or the other character that carries the message. The message, however, is not simple but complex. The moment one believes that the moral and political conclusion can already be drawn, it is called into question by the following scene.

The *Life of Galileo* could have been a tragedy because it fulfils two conditions of tragic drama. Galileo stands above everyone else in this play: he has grandeur, a modern grandeur, due to his achievements, not to his high birth. He is not evil but the opposite, a friendly and generous man, who has one overarching passion: a passion for knowledge and passion for progress. He believes in reason and he is possessed by a passion just as a tragic hero should be. He does not commit a crime, but he does commit a fatal mistake. His fatal mistake like that of Oedipus lies in his character. As an Epicurean he loves the good life, comfort and even luxury. The Republic of Venice can grant him freedom of research and protection from the Inquisition but not a high salary. He chooses income over freedom of research, Florence over Venice. He believes (as so many before and after him) that his reputation will protect him from persecution in Florence and in Rome. Moreover, he puts his faith in reason even more than in his own reputation. How can it be that people do not accept what is self-evident? Can't they see with their own eyes?

The issue in question is heliocentrism. In fact, heliocentrism was not Galileo's discovery, he just used it in a way no one else had used it before. The heliocentric worldview contradicted the Bible and Aristotle, the holy writ in philosophy and science in Galileo's age. Judging from the fate of Giordano Bruno, who was burned at the stake in 1600, nothing less than Galileo's life is at stake. Galileo trusted the new pope and believed that he could get away with teaching heliocentrism together with the traditional Ptolemaic-Aristotelian model, without hiding his own convictions. Despite his caution Galileo was indicted by the Inquisition and convicted as a heretic. He would have been burned at the stake like Giordano Bruno had he stood by his judgment. He revoked it, however. Given the authority of Galileo, this was a great victory for the Church against science. Galileo renounced his faith and his passion and thus the chance to become a tragic hero. The brilliance of Brecht's play is that it does not end here but in two encounters with his very first student, Andrea Sarti.

The first encounter ends with the frequently quoted exchange between the disciple and the master. Deeply disappointed in his master, Andrea laments, 'ill-fated are the times which have no heroes,' to which Galileo replies, 'ill-fated are the times which need heroes.' The writer, it appears, does not take sides. The second encounter takes place much later. Before leaving for the Netherlands, the land of freedom, Andrea visits the old Galileo in his confinement. It turns out that Galileo has secretly completed his greatest book *Discourses Relating to Two New Sciences* (1638) under the eyes of the Inquisition. Andrea asks Galileo for forgiveness; he had failed to understand that his master revoked the heliocentric worldview in order to be able to write his great book. This time Galileo takes the opposite position. Modern science, he answers, is no longer the work of a single genius. Had he not written *Discourses* someone else would have made the same discoveries. He has no alibi and he cannot be acquitted. Brecht leaves it to the reader or spectator to pass judgment, but above all to think over the conflict. The 'estrangement' paradigm – no empathy with the main character, no *catharsis* – is an invitation to the audience to feel and judge according to their worldviews and life experience.

Mother Courage was written directly before World War Two. It is a prophetic work. It takes place during the Thirty Years War. Mutter Courage and her children live from the war. She sells her commodities to whichever army is willing to buy them. At the beginning mother, two sons and a mute daughter draw the heavy cart laden in merchandise. At the end she draws the almost empty cart alone, since she has lost all three children to the war from which she lives. She seems to be without regrets. This is the only good 'pacifist' drama without ideology.

PART 3

The Endgame of Drama and Philosophy

1   Hegel and the End of History

Once again, I depart from the remark of Hegel that philosophy is like the owl of Minerva, it flies at dusk when darkness has already set in. This was not just a historical statement. The first philosopher of Athens, Socrates, was the friend of the last writer of tragedy, Euripides. Plato and Aristotle came later when no tragedy worthy of mention was written, epic poetry had disappeared even earlier. Hegel's metaphor is not just a poetic statement about ancient Athens: philosophy only appears when the developmental process of actuality (the final end of reality) has already been realised, it paints its grey in grey, it cannot tell the world how it should be. Hegel's philosophical metaphor means thus that our world cannot be renewed. Nothing remains for us other than to understand it. Hegel looks at his world rationally and therefore understands it. According to Hegel, we have arrived at the end of philosophy because we have arrived at the end of history. The last philosophy is the compendium of the history of philosophy. Hegel was the first to spell out the end of philosophy but almost immediately after it was declared by Marx and Kierkegaard, Nietzsche and Heidegger – four separate ends of philosophy. What did the end of philosophy mean for Hegel? As the World Spirit (the spirit of History) develops and takes different forms, philosophy changes and takes different forms. Philosophy is nothing but the spirit of a time expressed in concepts. All of these philosophies contain some truth, but only arrive at the Absolute Idea, the total determination of Being after going through numerous mediations to reach the Truth: the Whole is the Truth.

Just as all previous histories are both contained and negated in the present world, so in Hegel's philosophy all previous philosophies are negated and contained. Hegel does not claim to have created a new philosophy, for absolute idealism is nothing but a speculative re-creation (or re-telling) of the form of the history of philosophies. Anyhow, one cannot create a new philosophy: it would be impossible after the end of history. Hegel tells the story of philosophy at least twice: first in his *Lectures on the History of Philosophy*, and second in his *Science of Logic*. In the *Science of Logic* he presents the historical self-development of philosophical concepts, starting from Being-Nothing-Becoming. There is a parallel between the *de facto* development of philosophies and the self-development of philosophical concepts. Whereas the *de facto* development of the categories by different philosophers includes contingencies, the logical development is necessary and dialectical: first a category, then the negation of the category and finally the unification of both categories on a higher level and so on. Philosophical concepts develop from the abstract to the concrete. Finally, all philosophical concepts will be the total determinations of Being, the Absolute Idea. Hegel does not claim to have devised a new philosophy, rather that he understood all of them and could tell the whole story. The accusations that he believed that the Absolute Spirit dwells in his mind are utterly unjustified. For Hegel, philosophy ended in his age because his age was the end of history and he just happened to live at the end of history. His contemporaries had arrived at the end of the historical development of European history and thus at the end of world history. The end of European history leaves behind tragedy and philosophy. But these legacies are not corpses for they remain open to interpretation.

Hegel's statement about the ends of philosophy was perhaps his only statement with a huge following. Among radical philosophers, not many tears were shed for traditional philosophy. In the eleventh of his *Theses on Feuerbach* Marx stated that hitherto philosophers had only explained the world and that it is up to us to change it. This can be read as a criticism of Hegel's statement that philosophers of the present cannot tell the world anything about the future. This, however, Marx precisely wanted to do. He ridiculed Hegel, for whom history came to an end in the present. He took over Hegel's dialectics, yet believed that the continuation of history in the future was a 'law of history' as hard as the laws of nature. However, among the post-Hegelian radical philosophers Marx understood what Hegel meant by the end of history: not that there would be no conflicts, no wars and no suffering in the future, but that the present (modern) state of the world is the final state of the world. Marx corrected Hegel. The present capitalist state of the world is not the last state of the world but of class society. All class societies will be overturned and transcended by a classless society. All previous history will be followed by 'real history.' Marx also remained closest to Hegel in that in *Capital* he followed the method of Hegel's *Logic* and accepted the prediction that traditional philosophy had ended.

In the unpublished *Paris Manuscripts of 1844* the young Marx tried to conceive a new post-Hegelian type of philosophy in the form of *Dasein* analysis. (Marx's 'generic essence' is very similar to Heidegger's *Dasein*.) He soon gave up this new philosophical experiment in his eleventh Feuerbach thesis, setting an example for the kind of philosophy that was later called the philosophy of praxis. He then devised another philosophy: his materialist concept of history was a reversal of the Hegelian philosophy of history by changing the independent variable from the march of the world spirit to the development of the means of production. His conception was firmly based on the accumulation of empirically verified scientific knowledge, which was still far from reaching its final end and looked as it looks even now to be an unlimited, unstoppable development. Marx believed that it allows us to predict future developments and to discover both the laws of nature and laws of history. The associated idea that one can discover these laws only from the standpoint of the proletariat did not diminish the force of the belief in these laws. True scientific knowledge replaces philosophical truth and as such it replaces philosophy.

Nevertheless, the recognition that science and technology will progress in the future did not make Hegel's conception about the end of history absurd. Although the development of the means of production was in Marx's view the independent variable of historical development, this development itself was the story of the relations and modes of production and of different kinds of exploitation and class societies. The capitalism of the present will be the last class society. History up to now indeed ends with capitalism, the present and the last class society. What comes after? Classless society and communism, where there is no alienation, no state, no laws, no army, no market and everyone shares everything, according to his or her needs. This will finally be 'real history.' But what kind of history can that be if there is nothing historical left – no incentive to change, no dissatisfaction and no concept of justice or injustice? How can such a world change and develop if there is no motivation? Marx's real history is therefore not history at all, just like the thousand-year empire of Christ. There is no history in Marx's idea of the future in his most radical writings and Hegel wins the contest. Whether he meant it or not, Marx's end of philosophy is also the end of history. (Marx never speaks about a philosophy of true, real history and rightly so.)

Hegel's dictum about the end of philosophy was echoed by thinkers who rejected his work as a whole. Whether they also subscribed to his thesis on the end of history is another matter. For example, when Nietzsche speaks of the 'last man' this appears as corroboration, yet when he addresses the hope for the overman to come, this sounds closer to the Enlightenment and to Marx than to Hegel. The question is: what kind of philosophy can be practiced after the end of philosophy? I will return to this at the end. Marx understood Hegel well when he referred to capitalism as the last class society, the last society of alienation, reification and of history. If there is no society without alienation, then capitalism and reification are the end of the story. The well-known brief world history in *The Communist Manifesto* did not differ essentially from that of Hegel. He took over the dialectical method, describing history as a story of class conflicts, a story of constant negations followed by new affirmations. Both Hegel and Marx practiced the grand narrative of the history of humankind leading to the present and to modernity. If one disregards the motivational power of historical development (world spirit for Hegel, the forces of production for Marx) the two stories are more than compatible. Both begin with great Oriental cultures, continue with Greeks and Romans and finish with European modernity. Since modernity was invented in Europe, it is one with the grand narrative. The difference between the two lies not in the story itself, but in the judgment of the past of the present. Both Hegel and Marx speak about a progressive development, and both knew that one cannot compare different periods, only measure them quantitatively. Whereas Marx's speaks of the accumulation of knowledge Hegel talks about the generalization of freedom: that is, the quantity of knowledge or the number of free persons as the measure of progress. For both, modernity is the culmination of progressive development. What is the main difference? For Marx, there are two stages of modernity: capitalist and communist modernity. For Marx the latter will be the real culmination of historical development, whereas for Hegel the present is the culmination of progressive history, for there is no other modernity then the one developed in Europe since the Enlightenment. 'Here is the rose, here you dance!'

Hegel tells us to pick 'the rose from the cross of the present' but what kind of rose is it? After the French Revolution 'the world spirit on horseback' (Napoleon) is not that attractive. It is the world of prose – the poetry of life has no part in it. It is a world devoid of heroism, devoid of grandeur, a world of pettiness and even worse a world that produces and reproduces human scum (Pöbel). (What would he have said had he known the 20th century?) Still, there cannot be a more 'progressive' world than the one where everyone is free, where the slogan 'all men are born free' is at least generally accepted and where humans decide their future themselves. Hegel's description of modernity was based on the knowledge of his own times, and like all empirical descriptions of British and German reality (not actuality!) of the time, it soon lost its relevance (Hegel said exactly the same about Plato). As we see constantly in philosophy, the transcendental and even metaphysical conceptions maintain their basic influence after the changes of contemporary affairs.

Was Hegel right or wrong in his declaration about the end of history? If Marx is proven right, if by the laws of history a kind of modernity will necessarily emerge that differs essentially from all previous modes of production, Hegel was wrong. A kind of modernity where there will be no state, no laws, no market, and no wars and where nature will satisfy all human needs. If the Marxian vision turns out to be a utopia, a kind of transcendental idea, and the present structure of modernity is modernity in general and there is nothing after and above it, then Hegel was right. If for Hegel at the beginning one man was free and later a few persons and in modernity everyone is free, then how could history progress further. Only backwards. In fact, Marx also experimented with this alternative: socialism or barbarism.

It is a misunderstanding to reject Hegel's dictum by showing how many things have happened in Europe and in the world since Hegel – to speak only of totalitarian regimes and two world wars. Rousseau formulated this seeming contradiction clearly: 'All men are born free and they are everywhere in chains' – perhaps by now not everywhere but almost everywhere. Still, 'all men are born equally free' says the *Universal Declaration of Human Rights of the United Nations* and all states (and all tyrants) have signed it. The transcendental idea of universalism has won and together with it all the three logics or constituents of modernity: 1. science and technology 2. distribution by the market (capitalism) 3. freedom to choose political systems and institutions (Hannah Arendt was right: totalitarianism is as modern as liberal democracy).

These three constituents can be in conflict but one of them is decisive: the political. The fundamental sentence of modernity 'all men are born free' is a transcendental statement, but how and to what degree will it function as a constitutive practical idea (to speak with Kant) which will decide to what degree people are empirically free or not, even as far as the market economy or the development of science as technology is concerned. The capitalist economy produces inequality. A democratic welfare state will re-distribute national wealth to the losers, whereas a tyrannical state will redistribute to the loyal servants of the government. Re-feudalization is a possible option for welfare orientation. Still: all men are born free: modern tyrants and dictators are not the sons of kings and aristocrats; they are self-made men and women and elected by them.

All the three constituents of modernity were born in Europe and nowhere else. However, modernity is no longer European. *Homo sapiens* was born in Africa, humankind, however, is not African, High culture was born in Asia, but high culture is no longer Asian. Hegel could not have seen how fast this was going to happen (he only saw America and Russia as the two possible future great powers of modernity). It has happened rapidly and there remain only a few 'islands' of pre-modern ways of life in our world. The European idea of universalization has become reality. As with all transcendental ideas, the empirical world in which it takes root does not much resemble the idea. Ideas will never be completely realized, but they do transform contemporary empirical life.

What kind of history arrived at its end with modernity? It was the European history of progress from the times of the Renaissance on to modernity. The European idea of progress and its grand narrative included the old Asian civilizations and the ancient Greeks and Romans, who had, of course, no inkling of being links in chain of the progressive development of the world. However, they were incorporated into the idea of progress as the interest of the Europeans in the past and even the more remote past deepened. With modernity the preference for the 'new' and the nostalgia for the 'ancient' accelerated simultaneously.

What Hegel could not see but we can is that the generalization of modernity led to the shrinkage of Europe. One hundred years ago Europe was the dominating centre of the world. European war resulted in world war. One can imagine a European war in the present, but it would not result in a world war. Europe has become more and more insignificant compared to other domains of the globe. My conclusion is that Hegel was essentially right. Modernity as it developed in Europe is the end of history and that is the end of the world history invented, formulated, and created in Europe in the last 500 years.

In my interpretation of Hegel's vision of modernity I looked at the highest manifestation of Absolute Spirit in Hegel, namely, philosophy. However, I have not yet discussed the end of the earlier manifestations of Absolute Spirit: art and religion. Obviously, the end of history includes the full development of the state with all its institutions (law, family and so on), the market (together with its institutions property, contract and so on) and natural sciences – that is, the three constituents of modernity. The question is: why does the end of objective spirit result in the end of all three manifestations of the absolute spirit? Is this a kind of Marxian base-superstructure theory? One must not forget that the 'end' means arriving at the ultimate goal that includes everything that precedes it.

The 'end of religion' became a favourite philosophical topic after the death of Hegel. The hero of the day was Feuerbach. He was the first to reject Hegel's absolute idealism as a replacement for religion and made a strong case in favour of sensuality and sensuous experience as against logic and spirituality. One of his books, *The Essence of Christianity,* was embraced as the great credo of the day. According to Feuerbach, religion, especially Christian religion in creating the figures of God and Christ, is the product of the alienation of human essence. Humankind has alienated and worshipped its own essence and powers in those divine transcendental figures: Lord, Creator and Redeemer. Heine expressed it less theatrically and more historically. People go on Sundays to Church where they worship a dead God. Feuerbach had an enormous influence on the youth of his time. Men like Marx, Kierkegaard, Wagner and Nietzsche, to mention only a few. After some time all of them abandoned Feuerbach to make their own way. As Marx expressed it: everyone has to cross the 'fiery brook' (Feuerbach) in order to leave it behind.

To unmask religion and especially Christianity was on the theoretical agenda. If not just philosophy but all kinds of theoretical thinking express their age in concepts this is perfectly true about this period, the world of secularization, where the right to be agnostic, even to be an atheist was acknowledged as one liberty among the other liberties. A new aspect of modernity appeared in Feuerbach's reception. First, one can be a true Christian in one's individual private way, but, second, one can also live without religion. Third, and this is perhaps the most important, science has nothing to do with religion. If science and religious faith collide, one has to stand with science. This creed was at first exceptional and rebellious, later it became widespread. Darwin did not meet Galileo's fate. Even if Feuerbach's *Essence of Christianity* was not significant philosophically, it was up to date and this sufficed. Feuerbach's 'sensuous' philosophy was also meant as an attack upon Hegel, whose speculative philosophy, according to Feuerbach, was deeply Lutheran and just a new speculative version of the German religion.

I do not want to be accused of Hegel's rehabilitation, but I must briefly introduce his lectures on religion into our discussion. It is true that Hegel was influenced by Luther (as almost all German philosophers were) and was right when he insisted that the Reformation was an essential step in the development of the spirit of modernity. Yet, as readers of Hegel know, philosophy stood higher than religion in his hierarchy of Absolute Spirit, and for him the end of religion preceded the end of philosophy because of the dissolution of the congregation. Religion needs three constituents: God, the congregation and ceremonies of worship. When congregations dissolve, people can believe in God, yet religion is now at its end. There is thinking (*Denken*) but no devotion (*Andacht*), no spiritual and emotional associations. If religion is privatized, this is the end of religion. However, the end of religion is not necessarily the end of God in Hegel, since one can have one's own interpretation or vision of God. Even more (or worse?), there is no congregation in philosophy. The embodiment of the spirit is now only for a select few, for those having a speculative interest or talent. This is why philosophy has also arrived at its end.

Nietzsche was the most radical and the most influential exponent of Heine's *bon mot* about the dead God. To repeat: the madman runs among the crowd in the marketplace crying out the news that God is dead. (Don't you know? The Christian God is dead.) This is a telling metaphor, yet in fact Nietzsche refers in his poetic way to the same development as Hegel did. Modern men can carry on their daily life without ever referring to God, they can practice science and do not need God in their universe. Presidents or prime ministers are not 'God's anointed,' even if they sometimes take an oath on the Bible. Nietzsche is not rejoicing, simply sarcastic about the fall of the Platonic ascetic priest.

When declaring the end of religion or the end of philosophy and even the end of history Hegel was expressing his own present or the future of his present just as several other thinkers did after him. However, the end of art did not follow Hegel's prediction. We have to wait roughly 150 years for it to make sense at all. And that is a long time.

The modern conflict between the new and the old modified rather than replaced the contrast between high and low. Politics and taste could be assessed as up to date or obsolete, as modern or antiquated. Philosophy was no exception. In his lectures on the history of philosophy, Hegel cries out like a sailor 'Land!' when he arrives at Descartes. From now on we are at home. In modernity the new is constantly replaced by the newer, thus every new became sooner or later old. At the beginning the change was slow but in the 19th and 20th centuries it accelerated more and more rapidly. Philosophy did not stand apart as a spectator but took sides in almost all scientific controversies. Several modern philosophers (Descartes, Pascal, Leibniz) were also scientists in the modern sense, just as modern scientists like Galileo, Newton or Darwin were also philosophers.

Since the Enlightenment philosophers have also been taking sides in artistic questions. Rousseau, Diderot, Lessing or Shaftesbury in England took sides not only in literature but also in music and the fine arts. Aesthetics became a special branch of philosophy. The concept of 'taste' and the change of taste occupied a central place in the ongoing transformation of the concepts of the 'beautiful' and the 'sublime.' As the change in taste accelerated and the new was replaced by the ever newer, philosophers became more and more passionate partisans of one or the other new (sometimes old) 'ism' or of the idea of art above all 'isms.' Among radical philosophers Kierkegaard, Nietzsche and Freud were all involved in these art wars. We encountered above Nietzsche's involvement in 'the case of Wagner.' I also mentioned Kierkegaard's prediction that art will become more and more comic, given the comic character of the modern age. The ever-accelerating change in the spirit (taste) of the arts, especially in fine arts and in music (to a lesser extent also in literature) from the second half of the 19th century went together with the accelerating speed of discoveries (even new paradigms) in the natural sciences. Whether this similarity between the acceleration of discoveries in sciences and the rapid change in 'isms' in the arts can be explained by the importance of the technical aspect in music and the fine arts rather than in literature, I cannot decide. I can only state the facts. In film this connection is evident, yet it does not determine artistic quality.

It needs to be added that the increasing cult of the newest went together with the increasing cult of the oldest – again in the fine arts and in music – an essential difference between these arts and modern sciences. Here too literature followed its own agenda. Renaissance and Baroque music was rediscovered and given pride of place on the opera stage and the concert hall; Oriental, African and Oceanic artworks and everyday objects were hunted by collectors and museums, while at the same time Homer's epics or the Mahabharata remained treasures for the select few and the professionals. True, in high schools Virgil, Horace and Ovid were still being taught but in today's mass societies they are now outdated. Museums from the 19th century onwards followed the already generally accepted grand narrative. Historicism, as embodied in historical novels and historical dramas from early 19th century on, became at the same time the organizing principle of museums of fine art. Works of art were displayed in a historical (or quasi-historical) sequence.

In the fine arts various 'isms' followed one another increasingly rapidly: academism, realism, impressionism, post-impressionism, expressionism, surrealism, cubism, constructivism, Dadaism, as well as the several schools without an 'ism' like the Fauves, the Nabi or abstract painting. In music something similar took place, even if less fast and less dramatically. Philosophers of aesthetics promoted mostly the latest 'isms,' praising the greatest modernists for being revolutionary and abusing former 'isms' as reactionary. Some even promoted the new art genre of film. Painting ended up as white painted on white – and from here one could go no further, only backwards. In music Adorno declared the modernist Stravinsky an apologist of the bourgeoisie and prohibited the common chord as a 'lie.' Figurative painting of all kinds was declared out of date, along with harmony or melody in music. What did not happen in the sciences happened in fine arts and music. The running amok stopped. Suddenly everything or anything became possible in the fine arts and in music. The common chord returned in minimalist music; figurative painting revived. New genres like video or installations attracted attention. And this is exactly what Hegel predicted when speaking of the end of art.

To avoid misunderstanding: so-called post-modern artists create good and sometimes even great works of art. These artworks, however, are no longer European, they are global. They do not belong to the story that began in Egypt and ended in Paris. They are beyond this story, beyond and after the end of history. Post-modern works are created in Latin America, Asia, Africa, not forgetting North America. Despite their local colour they are first and foremost personal, individual statements. A single glance at a Venice Biennale will confirm this fact. Something very similar happened in music. Beside great post-modern Europeans composers in other continents now participate, while European classics (operas, concert music) are played all around the globe by famous non-European pianists, violinists, singers and so on. (The simultaneous globalization of entertainment together with high culture does not belong to my theme.)

The novel, especially the social novel, arrived only in modern times, at least in Europe (I have no expertise to speak about Chinese novels even though I like to read them). The first European novels were comic novels, followed by social, political or historical novels, sometimes with a 'happy ending' (marriage), sometimes with 'lost illusions.' From the beginning the novel was considered a 'popular' genre, read by a wider public, especially women. Although cheap books serving only light entertainment occupied a place in book production and sale from the beginning, literature was meant to be read by the many not just by the few. This started to change in the 20th century. Novel writers could not escape the general tendency of the acceleration toward the end of art and created great works in this spirit (Proust). They also made more or less successful attempts to leave traditional novel structures behind, e.g. starting at the end and going backward, eliminating the omniscient narrator or writing in a halfway private language (*Finnigan's Wake*). These novels appealed to a highbrow audience. Thus the world of novel writing became more and more divided between those who cherished the tradition and wanted to tell a story and those who wanted to 'overcome' realistic writing altogether in one way or the other. Some of the 'naïve' story tellers also became modern, not by renewing the form, what they rarely did, but by addressing actual issues, up to date topics (exploitation, poverty, human relations in general, women's issues, marriage in particular, and even wars, capitalist market relations, genocide, and sexual love). The new genre of the detective story also responded to the division of the genre. The thrill lost by highbrow literature was reborn in the 'thriller.' (One can see something similar in music.) Nevertheless, the genre of the novel, the latest fruit of European literature, came to an end almost but not entirely in the same way as in the fine arts. The genre became globalized. Significant novels are no longer written exclusively in Europe but also in Japan, China, Latin America, the Middle East and in Africa.

With his dictum about the end of art Hegel did not mean that there will be no works of art created in the future. Neither did the end of religion mean that no one will believe in God in the future. Hegel meant that the European story of art and religion has ended in modernity, the latter with Protestantism or – as others added – with the death of God.

2   Drama and Philosophy: The Endgame

I cannot repeat too often that tragedy and philosophy are European genres. They were born in Europe and died in Europe. European philosophy is taught nowadays in all the universities of the world just as Shakespeare and Ibsen are played across the globe (except for totalitarian states, where they are outlawed, together with many other things). But as with earthquakes the end of tragedy and the end of philosophy was and is also characterized by forceful aftershocks. These aftershocks are seemingly parallel only as far as the time of their appearance is concerned and not in their spirit or message.

The new modern genre of the novel was born in the form of the comic novel from Cervantes to Swift, later leaving the strong comic aspect behind. The comic aspect returned with the aftershock as far as high art was concerned, as we see after the First World War. Consider the works by Thomas Mann in the order of their appearance. *Buddenbrooks* (1901) is a traditional novel, *The Magic Mountain* (1924) works with symbolism and reflects on the first great crisis of European modernity, *Doctor Faustus* (1947) gets rid of the omniscient narrator and is filled with autobiographical self-reflections and monologues, just like Proust's masterpiece, while the unfinished *Felix Krull* (1954) and his last novel *The Holy Sinner* (1951) are comic, even absurd. Or, to go back a little in time, Musil's *The Man without Qualities* (1930–1943) is already a comic novel, some of Kafka's short stories and even his novels can be read as tragicomic works, but the breakthrough to the modern comic genres happened in Joyce's *Ulysses* (1922). In the genre of the comic-absurd short story Borges and Beckett stand out. The most significant tragicomic writer and classic of 'absurd drama' is Beckett. He worked for some time with Joyce and he excelled in 'absurd' comic novels before he turned towards drama. I mention in brackets that the three most significant 'absurd' dramatists (Beckett, Ionesco, and Dürrenmatt) came from the margins of Europe, Ireland (like Shaw and Joyce), Romania, and Switzerland. Just as the most significant 'absurd' short story writer, Borges, came from Argentina.

I dare to say that we witnessed the last significant blossoming of European drama after the two World Wars as reflections on an age experienced as absurd. In *The Immortal Comedy* I termed these dramas 'existential comedy,' since they centre around the fundamental concerns of naked human existence, deprived of all historical and temporal garments. Yet they can also be called absurd, given the quasi-dreamlike character of their plots. They resemble nightmares, both comic and tragic. Structurally, however, they do not follow dream logic. Their structure is actually Aristotelian since they rigorously follow the rules of the unity of time, place and story.

One of Beckett's most significant plays, *Endgame* (1957), is said to be a tragicomedy. What kind of a game is Beckett referring to? What is the game that comes to an end? The game of personal life? Yes. The game of historical life? Yes. The game of writing dramas or acting in them? Yes. (I know of only one other work that presents us with the 'endgame' in a similar dramatic triad, the Hungarian film by Bela Tarr, *The Turin Horse,* 2011.) Beckett's dramas are the endgames of the parallel history I have tried to trace. They are not just the latest but also the last great dramas of the genre originating in Athenian tragedies. This is why, I think, their main characters are symbolic. As puppet figures, circus clowns they are abstractions. We, the spectators, the readers, know the function of these characters, these human abstractions, just as well as we know the function of mythological characters. These existential dramas end with death, like tragedy, yet without the total devastation of life and the world of tragedy. They might be sad or even frightening but they are never tragic: rather a kind of twilight of the gods. Not a single character stands above the spectator or reader. They are all representations of different types of *homo sapiens* thrown into symbolic situations. These reincarnations are ridiculous, appearing to us as caricatures. Yet they are still human beings, one has to pity them while bursting out in laughter. Comedy 'larmoyante' and tragedy 'larmoyante 'are fused in one.

Waiting for Godot (1953), a drama Beckett termed 'tragicomedy,' was the first breakthrough, but with its quasi-repetition of the first act in the second act and its adherence to the three unities, it stands, as I suggested, in some sense closer to *The Cherry Orchard* than to *Endgame*. All this together has a tragicomic effect of pity and laughter in one. True, in *Godot* there appears already a third aspect beside laughter and pity, something that characterizes Beckett's later works: philosophical reflection. Reflection on the play, on the characters of the play and their fates, but also on the human condition in general. The two main characters Estragon and Vladimir are circus clowns, who present and represent major European themes: Don Quixote versus Sancho Panza; Vladimir dreaming of climbing the Eiffel tower and falling down like Ibsen's Solness; Estragon trying to hang himself like Papageno. Both, especially Vladimir, are forever waiting for Godot, while Godot sends his messenger angel to them twice, but he never comes.

Vladimir presents the best of the human race; he is the one who hopes and helps. He hopes to be saved yet he does not know from what. Is it from being born, he asks? The other 'pair' of the play are Pozzo and Lucky. Pozzo, another circus character, is an animal trainer and Lucky plays the role of an animal – and is treated like an animal. Vladimir is not only waiting for Godot; he also saves the mistreated Lucky and wipes away his tears. And the barren tree grows new green leaves overnight (as in *Tannhäuser*). Vladimir is saved. But from what, they both ask. From having been born. In the second part, during the repetition one thing happens: Lucky and Pozzo exchange roles. Human frailty, evil, goodness, hope, fear, friendship, and laughter – are they all together vanity or not? Beckett did not particularly like his great drama, obviously because of its not entirely hidden sentimentality, because of too much understanding and hope, even if it just remains hope. Perhaps also because it has a kind of mysticism, a last spiritual and poetic remnant of religious feeling. Of these nothing remains in *Endgame* or in *Happy Days* (1961).

Endgame is, as I already remarked, a title open to several interpretations. For example: when we die the whole world dies with us. We encounter here also two pairs. The old parents (Nagg and Nell) tied to one another and buried up to their shoulders in a pit. Their conversation is entirely banal. The contrast between situation and conversation could not be more grotesque. The old woman sometimes scratches the back of her old mate, and that is all. They reminiscence about their common past, banalities again, and they laugh – all is vanity in a stronger version. The second pair of *Endgame* is their son Hamm and his slave-servant Clov. How very Greek! The old King and the old Queen, the suffering son and the slave!

Hamm and Clov live between empty walls in a closed cellar-like place. (Are we all closed in our own world without able to see anything above or outside it, even if we try hard?) Hamm sits in a wheelchair, he is sick, he is unable to stand. There is a ladder in the cave to a single window. Only Clov, the slave, can climb the ladder to look outside: to see something or nothing? They are the last men in Nietzsche's sense. The metaphor is translated literally: 'Why do you keep me?' asks Clov. 'There is no one else,' answers Hamm. An unsolved riddle is built into the dialogues and monologues. Clov has to serve Hamm because he is punished for a crime, of which he knows nothing. Is it that everyone is a sinner? Clov tries to free himself from service, from his punishment or his sin. His first words in the drama are 'Fini, c'est fini, ca va finir, sa va peut-etre finir. On ne peut plus me punir.'

We find ourselves in an existential thriller. We can guess: perhaps repetition is punishment. Or life itself. As Clov remarks, life keeps raising the same questions: 'Pourquois cette comédie, tous les jours?' And Hamm's answer: 'La routine.' I do not know whether Beckett read Kierkegaard's *Repetition*, where he says that on the one hand repetition of the same is impossible and on the other hand that life is about repetition. But Beckett certainly knew Nietzsche's word about 'the eternal repetition of the same.' The dialogues between Clov and Hamm are only seemingly banal, since every dialogue implies the same philosophical question: why this banality? why this comedy? Clov finally liberates himself from service, his punishment, his sin. He leaves behind the dying Hamm. However, at the end, entering the grey nothingness, he still fancies he can see a faint and clouded image of a youth just appearing from afar. The messenger of Godot or a ghost?

The language of Beckett's plays, of his novels and short stories is a play of incongruent logic, puns, and surprising associations. Banality is always stylized. This is a tradition, frequent in Shakespeare, in relation to the socially and culturally low figures in comedies, whose language use is ridiculous or by chance wise. Hamm and Clov, Nell and Nag or Willie and Winnie in *Happy Days* are not simply ridiculous because their situation is not ridiculous, hence their dialogues become bizarre, surrealistic. According to Freud laughter is the manifestation of relief, but not here: here it is rather the manifestation of undigested anxiety. There is no redeeming laughter. The confusion of language is situated in an impossible nightmare, even if this nightmare is unlike a dream since the identity of place, time and character is preserved. The plays' language games (Wittgenstein) are distorted for the spectator, yet the characters play and understand them quasi-naturally. This incongruent use of language will be even more pointed in Ionesco. I am inclined to speak in the case of Beckett about constitutive humour, however, I would rather describe the spirit of Ionesco's plays as constitutive irony.

Ionesco makes fun from disorganizing language, like Joyce in *Finnigan's Wake*. However, he keeps the distortion understandable not just for the other characters but also for the reader or the audience. In *The Bald Soprano* (1950) the conversation between Mr. and Mrs. Smith is almost word for word taken from an English language reader. Of course, everyone understands the sentences as well as Mr. and Mrs. Smith but to hear 'normal' people talking like parrots is not just ridiculous, it is also horrifying.

With absurd or existential drama my history of tragedy comes to an end. And what about philosophy?

Post-Hegelian radical philosophies wanted to inspire and influence not just other philosophers but also the broader public present and future. Great philosophies never die. Latecomers can get inspiration from Plato or from Hume to the present day, not to speak of the eternal sources of thinking. However, the role that radical philosophies play in the 20th and 21st centuries is different. Their thinking is not only embodied in works of philosophy or in their schools, but also in the so-called 'isms,' movements, institutions organized around them. These 'isms' are not just different interpretations of the radical philosophers, they also draw new and sometimes contradictory conclusions from them. Kierkegaard, for example, became 'existentialism,' secular or protestant. Among the different interpretations of Marx there are some essentially philosophical (the best among them Lukács' *History and Class Consciousness*), some sociological and some political. From the works and practice of Freud various schools originated, some hostile to the others. Radical philosophies influenced the sciences, medical and social practices, political ideas and actions alike. They were used and frequently misused. Nietzsche was misused by the Nazis, Marx by the Soviets. Kierkegaard and Freud did not suffer such a dangerous reception, but their ideas and thoughts were frequently vulgarized in public opinion

Post-Hegelian radical philosophies remain our contemporaries, yet other post-Hegelian philosophers, mostly sons of the 19th century, are no longer our 21th century contemporaries. What about philosophies of the 20th century? (I omit academic philosophy from the discussion and will only discuss the philosophies that I think relevant to my history.) As an introduction, I need to recall that almost all significant philosophers of the last century declared either the 'end of philosophy' or referred to a serious 'crisis' of philosophy, of the sciences, or of European culture in general. I also need to add that the separation of several traditional branches of philosophy from philosophy continued in the 20th century. After the division of philosophy of nature into a variety of natural sciences and social philosophy, sociology, political philosophy and political science emerged. Economists ceased to be philosophers. Logic became mathematics on the one hand and analytical philosophy on the other. True, there are also movements in reverse. Some psychologists turned to *Dasein* analysis, others developed 'existential therapy,' while Hans Jonas turned back to the philosophy of nature.

The second half of the 20th century gave birth to new 'isms,' such as neopositivism, functionalism, structuralism, pragmatism. Philosophical schools and trends have always differed: otherwise they would not enter into debates. There are always certain common concerns, issues and problems they address, albeit differently. One can only have controversies if there are some common concerns and if one philosopher recognizes the ideas of the other as philosophical ideas, even if they are considered false. Between so-called analytical and so-called continental philosophy, however, there are no common concerns and they do not even recognize each other as philosophies. This is a new phenomenon among thinkers calling themselves philosophers and teaching in philosophy departments and the sign of near doom.

What are the common concerns in the most significant philosophies of the 20th century from phenomenology, hermeneutics, philosophy of language to philosophy of science? I enumerate a few, and to my mind the most significant of them:

1. How to get rid of epistemology, one of the major issues in philosophy since Descartes, or how to reform it.
2. How to overcome metaphysical systems or how to return to the original philosophy and to the pure source and beginning.
3. How to find a method or a language to get rid of both of the above-mentioned problems and still remain philosophers in a traditional sense.

4. Is the task of philosophy still to create a world, or just to reflect upon the world and reject all methods? Or just to reflect upon any typical manifestation or text in the present world?

20th century of philosophy started with Edmund Husserl, the founding father of 'transcendental phenomenology.' If Hegel's dictum that philosophy is our own time expressed in concepts needs proof, Husserl's philosophy is the proof. Although his philosophical 'founding idea' from his *Logical Investigations* through to *The Crisis of European Sciences* remained essentially the same, his philosophical attitude, including his understanding of the task of philosophy and of his own philosophy, changed dramatically. Husserl is reflecting directly or indirectly the dramatic changes in Europe from the peaceful beginning of the century onwards through World War I up to the victory of Nazism in Germany. Husserl's central programme is the destruction of metaphysics through the deconstruction of Cartesian metaphysics, yet in a way that permits him to preserve and to develop further the original message of Cartesian thinking. Husserl claimed to unmask or rather unveil the 'real,' hidden message of Descartes' *Meditations*. Husserl's ambition was to provide philosophy with the ultimate, absolute foundation (*Letztbegründung*), since only thereby can philosophy finally become a true science. Before Descartes it was not even attempted, after Descartes philosophy fell back into the metaphysical past by seeking a foundation outside thinking (an object, a source, a referent). Descartes' starting point was innovative and the most promising: radical doubt. Descartes put the existence of the whole world in brackets (*epoché*), coming to the conclusion that only one thing remained certain: that he doubts. It was at this point that Descartes abandoned his own radicalism. He identified the ego – wrongly – with the soul (the thinking thing) and reintroduced the internal/external relation and asked how the former can be adequate to the latter, that is, how can it be guaranteed that what we know is really there, that it exists, arriving at God as the guarantor. Metaphysics was thus restored. Spinoza, Leibniz and even Kant followed suit. British empirical philosophy up to Hume's scepticism, according to Husserl, followed the right path, but only transcendental phenomenology arrived at the point of radicalizing Descartes and providing philosophy with the solid self-foundation through which it becomes a strong science.

Transcendental phenomenology accepts Descartes' argument up to his '*epoché*,' however, it does not identify ego with the soul or anything inside or outside – but without relapsing into solipsism. Reason and Being cannot be divided. The question is not whether the world exists but how it exists for us. It exists for us together with all alter-egos, transcendental inter-subjectivity is simply given in the ego. In the experience of the ego others are present as real thinking beings. The so-called natural attitude is overcome through the 'phenomenological reduction' that transforms the transcendence of 'natural' consciousness (the 'other' is outside) into the transcendence within the transcendental ego (the 'other' is outside within the ego). This is the philosophical issue. The natural sciences prevail just as in daily life.

I will not write here the history of philosophy just as I have not written the history of tragedy. I only wanted to indicate how the old themes of epistemology (how can I know that what I know exists and how can I be sure that what I know is true, and so on) become obsolete in transcendental phenomenology. They became obsolete in all post-Hegelian philosophies and were replaced by other questions and answers. Whereas Husserl initiated the school of 'phenomenology' and the paradigm of 'inter-subjectivity,' Wittgenstein initiated the paradigm of language, the other school that dominated the non-analytical philosophical departments for decades. Wittgenstein wrote two philosophies. The first during World War I: the *Tractatus Logico-Philosophicus* and the second during World War II: *Philosophical Investigations*. Wittgenstein experts do not agree whether the message of the two books is the same and only the method is different, or whether the message is also different. The first interpretation can rely on the last sentence of the *Tractatus:* 'Wovon man nicht sprechen kann, darüber muss man schweigen' (Of what one cannot speak, one has to remain silent), whereas the second relies on Wittgenstein's preface to *Philosophical Investigations* where he contrasts his new philosophy to the old one. I will not follow the debate and rely mainly on his *Investigations*.

Every word has its meaning and this meaning is the object (*Gegenstand*) for which the word stands. That is, the meaning of the word is the object. All traditional questions of epistemology are made obsolete (as in Husserl). Metaphysical philosophy, Wittgenstein says, runs against the borders and the limits of language. And as far as the ego is concerned, the I does not belong to the world and is the limit of the world. Just as the eye cannot see itself, so the ego cannot grasp itself. Language is essentially ordinary language. Every language is a form of life. The form of life includes everything: customs, stories, actions, feelings, ideas and beliefs. To think a language is to think a form of life. Forms of life are characterized by multiple language games such as declaring, describing, ordering, doing, surmising, reading, giving advice, thanking, abusing, and praying. In fact, Wittgenstein enumerates all aspects of a way of life. A way of life is the world, since the world is always 'a' world, language and every language is the home of every unique world.

To digress for a moment: Wittgenstein's starting point and endpoint was ordinary language. The sentences quoted in *Philosophical Investigations* are not those of tragedy or serious dramas. Their language was poetic or stylized.

Un-poetic everyday ordinary language was normally spoken by lowly figures and by servants, vagabonds and the like. In modern absurd drama, however, the embodiments of the 'human condition' speak ordinary language, the language of *Dasein* and of 'care.' In absurd drama the language games are distorted by the speakers. They misuse words and meanings. The language games are inadequate to the situation. They are like jokes, yet they are not meant as jokes. In absurd drama it is not philosophy that runs against the limits of language but ordinary language and the common world. If one talks nonsense 'naturally,' the world is nonsensical. If one misuses language games in the sense that they are entirely inadequately to the situation, the world will be nonsensical, even if people in dialogue understand one another. The circumstances in which they understand one another is in itself nonsense. In *Finnigan's Wake* Joyce went to the edge of running against the limits of language. Beckett and Ionesco follow suit in a less extreme manner: the spectator needs to understand the nonsense as making sense, that is, as telling something important by being absurd.

It is obvious that in Wittgenstein together with epistemology the transcendental sphere is also abandoned. Yet contrary to Husserl, something of the Kantian spirit shines through, although one should remain silent about it and throw away the ladder on which one climbed up. Transcendence is not denied, only its conceptualization (its language) is ridiculed as a kind of nonsense: the remote reference to Kierkegaard is unmistakable. The Husserl scholar, Heidegger surprised us with an almost evident and very adequate solution in his major work, *Being and Time*. Although his approach remains close to phenomenology, his philosophical answer differs essentially from that of Husserl and also from the later answer of Wittgenstein's *Investigations* (Wittgenstein, however, could and did refer to Heidegger). Heidegger's answer is 'fundamental ontology,' where the term 'fundamental' means as for Husserl 'self-foundation' and ontology means the science (the logos) of Being.

Heidegger uses the metaphor of Nicolaus Cusanus: we humans are thrown into a world. Human being is 'Being in the world.' (Later in Sartre's variation in *Being and Nothingness* humans are thrown into freedom.) What is the world into which we are thrown? Things at hand and things to hand: ordinary language, rules, customs, rites, beliefs, things of use and, of course, language games, even if Heidegger does not use the word. Humans are thus thrown into temporality alias historicity: into a world, into a time and place, into a way of life, the life of 'care,' into finality and 'living towards death.' Who is thrown? *Dasein* (Being-here). (In Hegel's *Logic Dasein* is the finite being.) Being, according to Heidegger, has priority over *Dasein*, both ontologically and ontically. Metaphysics is thus 'forgetfulness of Being.'

Hannah Arendt translated *Dasein* as the 'human condition.' A telling translation, for the existentials of *Dasein* are those of every single and of all human beings. The existential-ontological statement concerning *Dasein* as 'Being in the world' may resemble realism, says Heidegger, yet it is different because it does not include the ambition to prove the 'reality' of the world. It may also resemble idealism, he adds, yet it is different because it does not attribute existence (being) solely to consciousness. Heidegger's farewell to epistemology is, in the last instance, simple, yet the elaboration of this evident solution, however, is far from simple since Heidegger loves metaphors and stories and he introduces new philosophical characters (categories that he calls fundamental concepts) and transforms others. His results are, however, similar at least in one respect to those of Husserl and of Wittgenstein: he too leaves epistemology and metaphysics behind.

Husserl's phenomenology influenced philosophy not only in Germany but also in France. Husserl's *Cartesian Meditations* were translated into French by Levinas, while Sartre in *Being and Nothingness* remained truer to the phenomenological method than Heidegger ever did. Husserl's phenomenology was a good starting point to leave behind metaphysics and to overcome epistemology. However, it did not offer an understanding of the 'human condition' and make a case or meaning for it. The problem was solved, if I may use this stupid expression, by fusing phenomenology with Kierkegaard's philosophy of existence. This happened in Heidegger's *Being and Time*, although he never admitted it.

Wittgenstein's *Philosophical Investigations* and some of the great innovations in theory of language (for example, Saussure) gave rise to a fashionable philosophy of language. (There are fashions in philosophy just as in everything else.) One spoke about 'the linguistic turn' that makes philosophy of mind obsolete for good (this did not happen, for example, in the midst of the 'linguistic turn' Searle's book *Intentionality* was published). Different branches of philosophy of language, such as ordinary language theories, flourished. One of them had a broader social and even political appeal: the discourse theory of Habermas and Apel.

Habermas called his theory 'universal pragmatism' and Apel called his 'transcendental pragmatism.' Their starting point was quasi-empirical, namely, that there exist human communities of people arguing rationally with one another. Therefore, one can presuppose a transcendental 'ideal community of argumentation' where every participant is in the same (social) situation and where they argue without time pressure and everyone can presuppose the truthfulness (*Wahrhaftigkeit*) of the participants' arguments (no personal or egotistic motivation). And truth is the consensus. Both, especially Habermas, propose different types of rational argumentation and ideal communities of participants: of knowledge, ethics, morality, etc. It is a kind of Kantianism translated into philosophy of language as philosophical foundation for liberal democracy.

The third dominating tendency of post-World War 1 philosophy is hermeneutics. The influence of hermeneutics is almost general. The theory of hermeneutics and some of its most sophisticated works and versions are present, moreover, in academic philosophy departments from literature, theology, sociology, psychology, the arts to history and beyond. Hegel said that after the end of philosophy comes reflection. Hermeneutics became this kind of reflection. Hermeneutics includes reflection on all the branches of the social sciences, on beliefs, knowledge, institutions, creation and dreams. Indeed, on all texts. György Márkus raised and answered the question, why there is no hermeneutics of the natural sciences. Philosophy of science is an important branch of 20th century philosophy insofar as it influenced among others some of the philosophies that I discuss. Among the philosophers of science Popper and Kuhn left an essential mark on philosophical public opinion.

Hermeneutical practices are far older than the modern theory of hermeneutics. Starting with Biblical hermeneutics, for example the Talmud, where various rabbis interpreted the Holy Writ. It is presupposed that the *interpretandum*, the Holy Writ, stands higher than all interpretations. It also happens that a philosophical text is regarded as 'holy' by other philosophers, as in some Aristotle commentaries or in Lukács' famous essay 'Reification and the Class Consciousness of the Proletariat,' where Marx's texts are treated as holy texts. In the cases of hetero-interpretation, where philosophers interpret for example significant artworks, this is always the case.

Gadamer, the main theorist and propagandist of hermeneutics, follows the most recent philosophical inheritance: the hermeneutics of Schleiermacher, Dilthey and Heidegger. And he does exactly what he teaches: he practices understanding of the other and texts of others. He avoids all rhetoric and he does not want to persuade but rather to understand a text, a way of life, and while understanding, mediating the message of those texts, those ways of life to his own times. The aim and the result is a 'fusion of horizons.' According to Gadamer, 'prejudice' is not identical with false consciousness or ideology, as it was for the Enlightenment, because they are 'there' (being at hand) and we are thrown into our world. We cannot survive without appropriating the tradition and living according to basic prejudices (the natural attitude) and using them and their language games. Without this new approach to prejudice hermeneutics would be impossible, for the reader of a text would otherwise remain outside the text, never entering it and never able to fuse horizons. So understood, hermeneutics excludes critical reading as well as rhetoric.

Hermeneutics as a theory is also a way of avoiding epistemology and metaphysics (like Husserl, Wittgenstein, Heidegger) and in the process it became more and more omnivorous. Philosophy obviously needed a blood transfusion, and hermeneutics offered the means to rejuvenate it by using the blood of others or the blood of their own ancestors. We understand the texts of others and we mediate them to our own age, to our burning issues and fuse horizons. That we can never succeed in this attempt is another matter. The blood transfusion can make use of the blood of our own philosophical ancestors (I term this auto-interpretation), or the blood of others – arts, institutions, sciences, religions (I call this hetero-interpretation). Interpretation means understanding in contrast to explanation (as the neo-Kantians suggested) but also reflection, while treating the text as a launching pad for personal ruminations.

It is not easy to distinguish auto-interpretation and hetero-interpretation. Let me refer only to Heidegger after his so-called *Kehre* (turning). In his first philosophy, in *Being and Time* he engaged in something similar to a systematic universal theory of the human condition, for which 'fundamental ontology' is the ultimate foundation. After the *Kehre*, however, he turned to hermeneutics in that almost all his significant essays were interpretations in the previously described sense of understanding. The *interpretandum* varied. It could be a single painting (for example, by Van Gogh) or even the artwork in general, a sentence by Anaximander or the concept of truth (*aletheia*) in ancient Greek philosophy. It could also be a few sentences of a poem by Hölderlin or ruminations about language as such. All those texts are mediated by Heidegger into his own philosophy. Heidegger's hermeneutical exercises, especially in cases of auto-interpretation as in his lectures on Parmenides, are not just mediations of the beginnings to the present and of his own philosophy but also indicate a philosophical-political programme. Heidegger did not trust the ability of phenomenology or philosophy of language to rejuvenate philosophy. According to his later works, everything had gone wrong with philosophy, perhaps already from the beginning in Plato. One has to start anew and return to original thinking (*anfängliches Denken*) for a new beginning, if at all possible.

The favourite source of blood transfusion was and still is art, works of literature, fine arts and music. The authors who are busy with this blood transfusion are aware of their destiny to serve as the rear guard, not the avant-garde. In philosophy interpretations are very rarely crowned with success. Academic books written on single philosophers, mostly on one or another of their 'problems' with a million footnotes and references, are works in philology, not in philosophy. One can get a chair of philosophy with them yet never broader recognition, not to speak of lasting fame. Books written for a broader audience bringing some philosophical issues closer to a thinking readership more closely resemble philosophy in the traditional meaning of the word. They contribute to the modern history of reception.

Fruitful hetero-interpretations enrich philosophical thinking. The first main source of successful blood transfusion was art, especially music and the fine arts. This practice was, of course, not new. We came across this practice in the times of the Enlightenment (Diderot, Lessing). These kinds of hetero-interpretations also have a practical purpose: to defend new works of art and reject some traditions. The function of Adorno's philosophy of modern music and Diderot's *Salons* resemble each other in purpose but not philosophically. Adorno belongs to those modern thinkers who turned against the Enlightenment. Lessing's rejection of French classic tragedy was unjust, so too was Adorno's rejection of Stravinsky's music, but both were unjust in order to make the case for a kind of art that expressed the critical spirit of their times, that is, for a philosophical purpose. Both were contributions to good philosophy. Not to push the comparison too far: the critical philosophy of Adorno was meant to be not only a critique of the present but also a rejection of the grand narrative of progress that Lessing stood for. Adorno and Horkheimer's famous philosophical pamphlet, *Dialectic of Enlightenment,* reversed the story of progress, of gains with some losses, into a story of regress and total losses. Ironically, among all philosophers of the 20th century, Adorno stands closest to the philosophers of the Enlightenment, even as far his chosen genres are concerned such as pamphlets, aphorisms, cultural criticism, storytelling, art and literary interpretation.

As is apparent in the case of Adorno, for whom the concept of 'reification' was central, several branches of hermeneutics were deeply influenced by radical philosophy, by Marx and Nietzsche and occasionally by Freud. The same can also be said about another significant philosopher of the 'critical theory' tradition: Walter Benjamin. His hetero-interpretations concentrate on literature, in a less militant and more poetic manner than Adorno, as for example in his writings on Goethe's novel *Die Wahlverwandschaften (Elective Affinities)*, on Baudelaire or on the Baroque *Trauerspiel*. Benjamin also defends new genres or at least reflects on them, putting emphasis on the technical reproduction of art.

In a posthumous two volume edition of the smaller works of Michel Foucault, one reads: *Ethics: Aesthetics, Method, Epistemology*. How come? Was he a traditional old-fashioned philosopher? Not at all. He was the son of the 20th century and he practiced hermeneutics both as auto-interpreter and hetero-interpreter. His interests were multi-focused. All traditional topics became the object of his philosophical inquiries, discovering in them non-traditional messages. He did not ask whether we can know the world outside or from inside, but rather how the question changes, how the epistemological attitude and inquiry change. He declined to offer a theory of truth yet asks the question: how is truth produced? He broadens the inquiry concerning power from the theory of the state or exploitation to the understanding of the 'force fields' and the omnipresence of power relations that remain unnoticed. He does not judge sexual ethics but is rather interested in their relations and their historical changes. The 'texts' of his hermeneutical exercise could be artworks, scientific discoveries, institutions, commonplaces and ordinary speech. He is an omnivorous hermeneut. Maybe this is why one can easily distinguish so many traditional philosophical topics in his works. He wrote on knowledge (techniques of knowing), on institutions (techniques of power), on the ethics of psychology (techniques of the self). We may say that he included subjective, objective and absolute spirit (and within absolute spirit, artworks, religions and philosophies) in the texts of his inquiry. A system? In a way it is! Foucault said we cannot overcome Hegel in his address on the occasion of occupying his Chair at the Collège de France.

I notice that I wasted the term 'omnivorous hermeneutics' since I wanted to spare this pun for Derrida, although there is little resemblance between Foucault and Derrida. Perhaps because I use 'omnivorous' in different senses: with respect to Foucault, I meant all philosophical themes, and with respect to Derrida all possible texts. One of his books is entitled *Deconstruction and Philosophy*. A more telling title would have been 'Deconstruction of Philosophy.' What Husserl and Wittgenstein initiated is accomplished by Derrida. Neither the transcendental ego nor language games are the stepping-stones of his philosophy. Texts are. In his *Grammatology* Derrida remarks that everything is text and interpreters keep discussing what he meant. He meant precisely what he *did*. Not any one selected text, not the Bible, Aristotle or Marx, nor even the book of nature but just texts. Take any text, by accident or on purpose, no matter, a statement of Aristotle or a scene from *Hamlet*, Plato's pharmacy or an interpretation of a painting by Heidegger, the letter of the Apocalypse, psychoanalysis, forgiving or friendship or the sacrifice of Abraham.

Dear readers, do not try to explain texts or to address their 'problem' and their 'solution.' Do not ask whether they assert or deny, whether the author (who is the author anyway?) says yes or no, whether he or she agrees or disagrees and what his or her standpoint is. There are no standpoints and no messages, since standpoints and messages deconstruct themselves as you are reading them. No final results and no final consequences can be drawn. Every text is a goldmine. As one reads Derrida, hidden aspects of a text come to light with him and through him. Words, thoughts, relations one has never noticed are suddenly illuminated in Derrida's text, and soon something else, it goes on and on. The text that is deconstructed is always reconstructing itself and one never arrives at the end unless Derrida (the author?) stops or because the lecture runs out of time. The only thing that comes from the outside is the limit – perhaps the ultimate limit of the text reader's life. Whenever I discussed a work by Derrida with my students, they asked the obvious question: what did he want to state, what is his standpoint, his solution? I had to answer: you cannot read Derrida in this way, for he does not make such statements. He is presenting a chain of never-ending deconstructions of the text, of a never-ending understanding, just as understanding never ends.

Derrida says that the text deconstructs itself, but this is his exaggeration. He lets the text deconstruct itself, but the text would never do it without him or some other person. If you try to engage in deconstruction, you misjudge the task itself. Deconstruction is not a method everyone can learn and apply as Derrida did, it is personal. This was misinterpreted by Richard Rorty when he termed Derrida's philosophy a 'private' philosophy. Derrida was hurt, with justification: no philosophy is private. Just as there can be no private languages, there can be no private philosophy. However, personal philosophy exists. In fact, nowadays almost all significant philosophies are personal. There is no Derrida school since he died. Derrida lives in his texts and he was a genius at understanding texts. Consequently, he is the author and the owner of his own philosophy. In letting the texts deconstruct themselves, his works are full of astonishing conceptions, exciting discoveries, new ideas and new ways of thinking. One can always think them over and work on them. Derrida's deconstruction of philosophy is a philosophy. It is in my view the last philosophy, the long good-bye to this European genre born roughly two and a half thousand years ago in the small city of Athens. We have nothing new to say.

Philosophy is its world expressed in concepts. Philosophers are sometimes, not always, conscious of it. The majority of 20th century philosophers are. Moreover, most of them also directly reflected on the issues of their times. The reception of radical philosophies (Marx, Nietzsche) turned in this direction. Thus, some representative thinkers in phenomenology, philosophy of language and hermeneutics registered 'decadence' and 'decline' as recent significant losses. (Even some philosophers of science think the same.) Spengler's *Decline of the West* was widely read and discussed. Adorno and Horkheimer's *Dialectic of Enlightenment* was praised, even if not entirely understood, by the chosen few. In different periods of European history philosophers detected or saw signs of decline or even of collapse or catastrophe. The *Decline of the West* and similar stories are versions of the grand narrative. Instead of universal progress they talk about regress. The idea of the 'repetition of the same' is comparable. According to this story, every culture is born, after childhood it enters its youth, arrives at manhood and reaches its peak of development, then comes old age and finally death. This happened with Egypt, Babylon, Athens, and Rome – and will happen with us. Especially widespread is the comparison with Rome. Hegel too experiments with cultural ages, yet old does not mean for him the end of life, but the end of history as the ultimate goal of historical development.

Forget biological comparisons. The Europe of today does not resemble ancient Rome. The declining Rome was surrounded by 'barbarians,' who had no idea about Roman culture, past or a present. They destroyed libraries and works of art and started a culture of their own, almost (but not entirely) from scratch. The end of history, in my and in Hegel's understanding, does not mean decline but that Europe reached the peak of its self-development and having exhausted its possibilities has arrived at modernity. Modernity has not died, it has become almost universal, conquering almost the whole planet. At the end of history – its own conception – Europe has lost its central place as a political-social power and also its place as the creator of high art and philosophy. The grand narrative is finished.

The feeling of doom was at first experienced and described as a crisis. A crisis can have two contrary results. The sick person either dies or become healthier than before. Husserl, who stuck to a non-political, absolutely scholarly scientific approach, wrote in 1935 *The Crisis of European Sciences and Transcendental Phenomenology*. This 'strong' scientist asked the question whether we can live in a world where the historical chain of events is nothing but an illusion of progress, followed by bitter disappointments. For Husserl, the modern scientist can live in this world if he fulfils his vocation: to participate in the struggle around the meaning of being human. It requires us admitting that the rationalism of the 18th century Enlightenment is an illusion. Irrationalism was the response to this illusion. Nevertheless, he continues, philosophers should not give up the claim to universalism. Nietzsche's shadow reaches far. There is no philosophy without the contrast between the transcendental and the empirical. The transcendental sphere (the 'true world' as Nietzsche said) is not the world of experience but of thought, of the function of thinking we call reason. To repeat Nietzsche's story, if we destroy the other, the second world, we destroy the first too and that is the end of philosophy.

Husserl was not the first to ring the alarm bell, but he was the first philosopher who spoke in the name of a strong science. He expressed the feeling that with the end of philosophy, the end of tragedy and the end of history, all histories have ended and that together with our world everything is dying. The human world that had dominated the scene of absolute spirit, European culture itself, is at its end. Just as absurd drama occupied the theatre, hopelessness characterized more and more philosophy. As in Beckett, they were waiting for

Godot, who never came. In philosophy Marxists waited for the end of alienation and the just society that never came. Just as a kind of angel appears in Beckett on the remote horizon even at the moment of doomsday, in the mind of Heidegger only a new god can save us, and in the mind of Benjamin, for whom history was not a progressively constructed building but a heap of ruins, the Messiah appears in the redemptive imagination.

In this endgame, tragedy and philosophy meet one another again: the end of tragedy and the end of philosophy as the end of the world in which they were first born. First in Athens, then in the whole of Europe, where they flourished – with some interruptions – for more than two and half thousand years. They now end their life together in the modern world, carrying the remote hope of redemption. Yet, the Redeemer is unknown.

Conclusion

In the 21st century one can again raise Husserl's question: can one live in a world where the chain of great illusions is always followed by the chain of great disillusionment? Does it make sense to be engaged in philosophy or in writing plays? And if yes, why and how? And finally: has the spirit of universalism disappeared for good in modernity? To answer Husserl's question first. I think that in the 21st century Europeans – perhaps also people worldwide – have abandoned the great illusions and that therefore we will not end this time in great disillusionment.

The kind of acceleration of change witnessed in European modernity continues nowadays only in sciences and technology. We cannot know how long this will last since everything is finite. Universal progress ceased and the great narrative has come to its end, while the idea of universalism has been realized, even if not in the desired way. The 'ruse of reason' is still at work. We do not embrace millions and do not kiss the whole world. Ideas are and remain the ideas of reason and have never become empirical. Modernity is by now global and in this sense universal. All governments signed the Universal Declaration of the United Nations that all humans are born free. Everyone is free on paper. Enlightenment has won – but did it?

Let us consider the three constituents or logics of modernity: 1. primary distribution of people, goods, services etc. by the market 2. development and application of science and technology 3. the option to choose political rule, institutions, types of governments and the form and character of the state. In the case of the first and the second constituents (the market, science) there are no real alternatives, although their internal logic can be kept more or less under control or influenced by the third constituent of modernity: the character of the political institutions and the degree and the weight of liberty within society and the state. For here, in the case of the third logic, greatly varying political institutions, governments and political rule are possible. To enumerate a few: liberal democracy, mass democracy, despotism, military dictatorship, civil dictatorship, autocracy, totalitarianism.

I cannot repeat frequently enough: modernity is founded on freedom, but freedom is a foundation which does not found. As Rousseau put it almost three hundred years ago: 'all men are born free yet everywhere they are in chains.' Modernity is based on freedom, yet this foundation does not found a constitution or a set of rights. The end of history and the end of the grand narrative do not end the contestation of freedom. Since the last century the theoretical and practical interpretations of freedom are at stake. All the essential conflicts are rooted in the contestation of freedom.

Take the first logic of modernity: no one is free to abolish the market's function as the primary distributor of men, goods and services. Secondary distribution, the redistribution of the wealth in any state or nation is possible, it depends on politics, on the quality, measure and character of liberties in a state and hence how and in whose interest it happens. Regarding the second logic of modernity, no political system can stop scientific and technological progress without preparing its own (short or long term) doom. Yet, political institutions can directly influence priorities of scientific research and technological application, they can guarantee freedom for research and limit the influence of private or ideological (dictatorial) interest, thereby defending the second main value of modernity, life.

The 'battlefield' of modernity is not about the dream of earthly paradise or utopian illusions or the useless fight against the first or the second logics of modernity, it is about the ongoing contestation of liberties in which the quality of life of men and women is continuously decided and defended. The continuous defence of the institutions of liberty is the foundation and the measure of the 'good life.' The interpretation of freedom both theoretically and practically constitutes the stability or instability of the institutions of liberty in the continuity of the absolute present. How many times have we ridiculed Hegel because of his sentence that the state is the embodiment of God in history, that the freedom of all became 'flesh' in the state, not in the utopia to abolish it. However, if we look around our globe we have to come to the conclusion that he was right. Only liberal democratic states can guarantee liberties to all, to the extent men and women are ready to defend them. Only a liberal democratic state is able to correct the injustices of the market and defend against the eventual dangers of science and technology. The end of history is not the end of wars, conflicts, dictatorships and relapses into barbarism. It just offers the means to avoid and to fight against them.

Tragedy and philosophy were both born in Athens and both were born from the spirit of freedom. Not from the spirit of accomplished freedom, but from the spirit of the constant contestation of freedom on the foundation of Athenian democracy. They were born from this spirit independent of whether they were friends of democratic institutions or not. Even those who were not friends of the Athenian democracy were, at least in one sense, friends of liberty, since they defended after Socrates free speech and free opinion and free judgment against the majority. The end of philosophy is not necessarily the end of the spirit of philosophy as born from the spirit of democracy. If we accept Hegel's dictum that philosophy is nothing else than our age expressed in concepts, this will also be expressed in the spirit of the age.

Given that no utopia is going to be realized and humankind perfected, there will be no epoch-making new philosophies, no new history of philosophy. However, something, the backbone of philosophy will remain: critique. Criticism of empirical reality from the standpoint of transcendental ideas the way Socrates practiced it. Instead of the marketplace there are several other means to ask questions of our contemporaries and to confront them – not with The Truth – but with the necessity of self-reflection and with the ability to think and to understand. As Kant suggested, we need the ability to think with our own mind and also to think from the standpoint of another, to think consistently in order to accept and present a conviction one considers to be true. Philosophers after the end of philosophy are no less talented than their great ancestors, even though the age does not offer them room or space for fundamental innovation, for system building or a new perspective. It may serve as a consolation that the practice of philosophy will not be less dangerous. Thinking with one's own mind always remains dangerous, since it makes both the tyrants and public opinion uneasy.

For the last time let me return to the end of the grand narrative. Tragedy disappeared. But what about theatre? And what about drama? Is Beckett's *Endgame* the end of drama? Philosophy and tragedy are European literary genres. No other literary genre or art is European. When Hegel speaks of the end of philosophy and the end of history, he also speaks about the end of art. The grand narrative of Hegel and not just of Hegel included the world history of art. I highlighted earlier the surprising phenomenon that at the very time that the end of philosophy was being declared (from Marx through Nietzsche to Heidegger) the arts, the creation and the reception of art, underwent a process of unprecedented change: one 'ism' followed the other in the short story of 'modernism.' This time is now over. This is why they speak of post-modern art. The expression post-modern is frequently understood as meaning not just the end of modernism, but also the end of a historical period termed modern. This is a misunderstanding; the opposite is the case. Post-modern art is the art of ripe modernity. In a world where everyone is free, everything is art. Yet just as among all the governments, which signed the statement that all men are born free, there is liberty only in a few of them, so when everything is art only a small part will become timeless. This is not due to 'progress' in art history but is a reflection of the individuality of artworks, of their charisma and appeal.

Only tragedy and philosophy are European genres, but all the other genres were practiced in Europe and in several other cultures as well, including wisdom literature and theatre. So-called post-modern genres are created and practiced everywhere in the world. As modernity became global, that is universal, so too did post-modern art, like science and technology and the market. Only one thing is not globalized: politically institutionalized liberties. Democracy was invented in Europe; liberalism was also invented far later in Europe. The sentence that all humans are born free was born on this tiny continent as a philosophical idea and spread to its former colonies. Yet Europe betrayed and almost killed its own child in the most vicious ways by initiating two World Wars and inventing and establishing totalitarian dictatorships. European history has ended, since the grand narrative, this very European innovation, ended by being realized. Europe has accomplished its self-created historical mission and is now over. Yet it is not the apocalypse and not the end of the world, as it was imagined by outstanding European intellectuals.

I mentioned apocalypse, this is a religious tradition. The Hegelian narrative about the end of history includes the end of religion. I think, however, without justification. According to Jan Assmann, only monotheism can be called a religion. Why? Because all other religions, particularly the polytheistic, belonged to the cultures in which they flourished. When the cultures died, so too did the religions. As Schiller expressed it in his poem *The Gods of Greece*, Greek gods became aesthetic objects; we enjoy them as statues but we do not pray to them. Monotheistic religions are, referring again to Assmann, by contrast culturally indifferent. Jewish, Christian and Muslim religions could live and flourish within entirely different cultures. Moreover, as far as religion is concerned Europe had very little fantasy. All the great religions were invented in the Middle East and Asia. Protestantism as an originally European religion was just the accommodation of Christianity to modernity. The end of history is the end of religion only in the sense that no new universal religion will be born, not in the sense, that is, of universal atheism or universal secularism. Religions will assimilate and accommodate to different cultures as they always did, while in addition cultures may create their own local cults.

This can also be said about philosophy, just as about the end of the idea in all its variations. One is only justified in speaking about the end of something if one already knows the beginning of the new. The end as goal is only a goal if it is created or posited by someone. Hegel said that God (the World Spirit) invented the story he himself told. To my mind, Europeans invented the story at the beginning of modernity and closed it with the self-accomplishment of modernity. We are not in a position to look beyond it. Or, as Wittgenstein said, we threw away the ladder on which we climbed to this point. The European past lives in the memory of tragedy and thinks itself in the history of philosophy. Yet Europe lives in the present: it is present in the embodiments of the great European idea, in the institutions of liberty, in Europe's founding source: the idea of Freedom. The most difficult task still remains ahead.